"I have a passion for people to see and savor the God of the Bible, and a corresponding frustration when I see the hurt, loss, and lack of confidence that accompanies a lack of biblical literacy. That's why I'm glad you are holding this book. Jen Wilkin takes knowing the God of the Bible seriously. She is one of the better Bible teachers I've had the opportunity to hear. Her approach in teaching people how to grow in their knowledge of the Scriptures is accessible and helpful regardless of whether you have been a Christian for decades and feel like it's too late for you or you are a young believer who is hungry to know and understand the God of the Bible."

Matt Chandler, Lead Pastor, The Village Church, Dallas, Texas; President, Acts 29 Church Planting Network

"I found *Women of the Word* to be so practical in the way it demystifies serious Bible study. Too many people—men and women—opt for just reading a few verses and hoping for some inspiration, rather than discovering the meaning of the text in the sweep of God's redemptive plan. *Women of the Word* will help anyone who reads it to find their way deeper into the Word of God without having to be seminary educated, a genius, or even an especially good student. My only caveat is that I wish the title didn't make it hard for men to read . . . they need it, too."

Kathy Keller, Assistant Director of Communications, Redeemer Presbyterian Church, New York City, New York

"I've seen eyes misty with tears as women come to understand for the first time that the Bible is actually, literally God's Word. What great mercy we have been shown—that the Creator who spoke everything that ever was into existence would give us his Word. Jen Wilkin knows this mercy in the core of her being. She has tasted and seen God's goodness in his Word, and she doesn't want a single woman to miss it. Read *Women of the Word* with your Bible open and your friends alongside you. Think of this book as a maître d' of a Bible study banquet—have a seat, here are your utensils, dig in, and *enjoy*."

Gloria Furman, Pastor's wife, Redeemer Church of Dubai; mother of four; author, *Glimpses of Grace* and *Treasuring Christ When Your Hands Are Full*

"Jen lives what she teaches. Her servant heart in unpacking the Scriptures as well as her affection for the women she is teaching is evident the moment you meet her. I'm so glad she was obedient to the Lord's call to write this book! It has served to clear the fog in my heart and mind when it comes to studying God's Word, and I absolutely cannot wait to purchase many more copies for the women in my life who I know will love it too!"

Bethany Dillon, singer/songwriter

"This book responds to the feelings-driven, me-centered approach that has too often dominated our study of the Scriptures. Jen encourages women to grow in knowledge of the Word in order to know our Lord. She speaks out of her own joyful and growing experience of learning to dig in. May her voice be joined by many others!

Kathleen Nielson, Director of Women's Initiatives, The Gospel Coalition

"Reading the Bible can sometimes seem daunting. There are difficult passages, many interpretations, and often so little time to read thoroughly. Jen Wilkin recognizes this and provides tools to help us navigate it all. *Women of the Word* gives us a blueprint for Bible literacy. If we want to know the God we love, we must engage our minds and know his Word where he reveals himself. Wilkin's tools may be new for some, but the effort will be worth the reward. Ultimately, it's about seeing and savoring our Savior."

Trillia Newbell, author, *United: Captured by God's Vision of Diversity*

"Jen Wilkin's book is written with a winsomeness and warmth, which makes it easy to read. But she also writes with clarity of purpose that rightly pushes the reader to want to read God's Word well. The bottom line: this book encourages women to know God better by developing good habits of reading his Word. Amen, sister!"

Jenny Salt, Dean of Students, Sydney Missionary and Bible College

"How can we go deeper than a little dabbling in the Bible for inspiration? Jen Wilkin shows us how in this must-read for every woman interested in teaching and leading Bible discussion groups in your church."

Nancy Guthrie, Bible Teacher; author, Seeing Jesus in the Old Testament Bible study series

Women of the Word

How to STUDY *the* BIBLE *with*
Both OUR HEARTS *and* OUR MINDS

◆

JEN WILKIN

WHEATON, ILLINOIS

Women of the Word: How to Study the Bible with Both Our Hearts and *Our Minds*

Published by Crossway
1300 Crescent Street
Wheaton, Illinois 60187

Cover design: Connie Gabbert

Cover images: Shutterstock

First printing 2014

Printed in the United States of America

All emphases in Scripture quotations have been added by the author.

Trade paperback ISBN: 978-1-4335-4176-6
ePub ISBN: 978-1-4335-4179-7
PDF ISBN: 978-1-4335-4177-3
Mobipocket ISBN: 978-1-4335-4178-0

Library of Congress Cataloging-in-Publication Data

Wilkin, Jen, 1969–
Women of the word : how to study the Bible with both our hearts and our minds / Jen Wilkin.
pages cm
Includes bibliographical references and index.
ISBN 978-1-4335-4176-6 (tp)
1. Bible—Study and teaching. 2. Christian women—Religious life. I. Title.
BS600.3.W555 2014
220.071—dc23 2013044796

Crossway is a publishing ministry of Good News Publishers.

VP 24 23 22 21 20 19 18 17 16 15
18 17 16 15 14 13 12 11 10 9 8 7 6 5

To Jeff, who knows me best.
You give me courage. Psalm 34:3

Contents

Foreword

When the Holy Spirit opened my eyes to believe, it was like being run over by a train. I fell in love with Jesus that night and have yet to get over it. But although my heart was aflame, my mind was empty. I asked hundreds of questions that night and in the following days.

In God's gracious providence, he put a man in my life who was willing to teach me early on what the Bible was. This quote from Ed Clowney encapsulates what I learned in those early days:

> There are great stories in the Bible . . . but it is possible to know Bible stories, yet miss the Bible story. . . . The Bible has a story line. It traces an unfolding drama. The story follows the history of Israel, but it does not begin there, nor does it contain what you would expect in a national history. . . . If we forget the story line, we cut the heart out of the Bible. Sunday school stories are then told as tamer stories of the Sunday comics, where Samson substitutes for Superman; David becomes a Hebrew version of Jack the Giant Killer. No, David is not a brave little boy who isn't afraid of the big bad giant. He is the Lord's anointed. . . . God chose David as a king after his own heart in order to prepare for David's great Son, our Deliverer and Champion."[1]

Over the last twenty years, the Holy Spirit has used the Scriptures to encourage me; rebuke me; shape my marriage, my parenting, my approach to money, and my outlook in the midst of tragedy; and to repeatedly draw my eyes to the One whom the Bible is about. I find in my heart a passion for people to see and savor the God of the Bible, and a corresponding frustration when I see the hurt, loss, and lack of confidence that accompanies a lack of biblical literacy.

That's why I'm glad you are holding this book. Jen Wilkin takes knowing the God of the Bible seriously. She is one of the better Bible teachers I've had the opportunity to hear. Her approach in teaching people how to grow in their knowledge of the Scriptures is accessible and helpful regardless of whether you have been a Christian for decades and feel like it's too late for you or you are a young believer who is hungry to know and understand the God of the Bible. Her 5 P's of *purpose*, *perspective*, *patience*, *process*, and *prayer* will serve you well in the days, weeks, and months ahead.

I am confident that as you learn and practice Jen's Bible study methods, you will be enthralled by both the Bible's stories and its story, and you will be forever changed as you come to know the Hero of that story.

Christ is All,
Matt Chandler
Lead Pastor, The Village Church
President, Acts 29 Church Planting Network

Acknowledgments

I am grateful to Collin Hansen and Dave DeWit for believing I had something to say, and for giving me a means to say it. You both knew I was a writer before I did.

To my faithful "freditors"—Lindsey Brittain, Kindra Grider, Lori Kuykendall, and Kristen Rabalais—thank you for reading all the clumsiest versions of my thoughts and gently helping me to be a better communicator. I value your edits, but I value your friendship more.

Emily Spalding and Sally Sturm, "free therapy" is a bit of an understatement. I love you both.

Tara Davis, thank you for giving me back the Oxford comma, and for untangling my sentences with patience and grace. Gloria Furman, you generously read my manuscript in the weeks after your fourth child's arrival. I know first-hand you had other things to do, and your encouragement was a priceless gift.

Matt Chandler, you extended friendship and unqualified support of my ministry and message. Thank you for being my pastor. Kent Rabalais and Sara Lamb, your willingness to help me balance my role at The Village Church with my writing commitments kept me sane.

Matt, Mary Kate, Claire, and Calvin, you are my favorite children in the world. By giving me space to write and helping me keep our house standing you have partnered with me in ministry. Let's not eat frozen lasagna for a while.

And to the women of Flower Mound Women's Bible Study, whose hunger and thirst for righteousness has been an ongoing inspiration to keep my hand on the plow, thank you for sticking with me and for loving God with your minds. You are a precious weekly reminder that this work matters.

Introduction

How do you move a mountain?
One spoonful of dirt at a time.

Chinese proverb

This is a book about moving a mountain. The mountain is my own, though I admit that I overlooked its existence until I was in my twenties. I suspect it may be your mountain as well, but you'll have to decide that for yourself. Unlike Pikes Peak or Kilimanjaro, this mountain does not immediately announce itself to our vision—it takes time to see. Thankfully, unlike a real mountain, this one can be moved. That's a good thing, because there is something unspeakably beautiful to behold on the other side.

If there were such a thing as a church pedigree, mine would read "mixed breed." I spent my childhood searching for a church to call home, following one or the other of my parents (who divorced when I was nine) to their current places of worship. I logged significant time in seven different denominations, during which I went to Sunday schools, vacation Bible schools, youth groups, and retreats. I was sprinkled as an infant and immersed as a teen. I sang hymns from hymnals set to organ music, and I sang praise songs from projection screens set to guitar music. I learned to raise my hands in worship, and I learned to keep them at my sides. I heard sermons read in monotones and sermons shouted with vigor. I learned the cadence of creeds and liturgies as well as the cadence of tambourines and dancing. I learned to have a "quiet time" and memorized numerous Bible verses to earn a free trip to summer camp. I learned how to share the gospel with my lost friends. I was a church kid—albeit a kid of many churches—and I could give answers to Sunday school questions that made my teachers beam with pride.

In college I continued my denominational travels, reading devotional books and attending Bible studies to fan the flames of my faith. By my senior year I had been asked to lead a study. But I carried a secret not uncommon to people with my background: I didn't know my Bible. Sure, I knew parts of it—I remembered stories from vacation Bible school and I could quote verses from all over the New Testament and Psalms—but I didn't know how the parts that I knew fit with each other, much less how they fit with the parts I didn't know yet. Looming in my peripheral vision was a mountain of biblical ignorance that was just beginning to cause me concern. Though I treasured what I knew, I was growing troubled by what I did not know.

Spending time in all those different churches had taught me the worrying truth that all pastors had much to say, but not all pastors were saying the same things. Who was right? Was there a rapture or not? Did God have to answer our prayers if we prayed a certain way? Did I need to be baptized again? How old is the earth? Were Old Testament believers saved differently than New Testament believers? For the most part, my teachers sounded equally convincing. How could I know who was properly interpreting the Bible and who was teaching error? Learning firsthand the painful fallout of wrong teaching sparked in me a desire to know for myself what the Bible taught.

Marriage and motherhood increased my sense of urgency to learn, revealing how ill-equipped I was to fill those roles in God-honoring ways. But I didn't know where to begin to fix the problem. It seemed beyond obvious that if God had given us his revealed will in the Bible, I should be spending more time trying to know and understand it. But the task seemed overwhelming. Where was I supposed to start? And why weren't the things I was already doing making the problem discernibly better? How was I supposed to move the mountain of my biblical ignorance?

The answer, of course, was gloriously simple. The answer was "one spoonful at a time." Thankfully, someone gave me a spoon.

I admit that I went to my first women's Bible study looking for adult conversation and coffee cake, not necessarily in that order. The siren-call of free childcare was more than this young mother with a three-month-old could resist, so I went to get out of the house and get back into the land of the living. What I found was a thing of sweetness: a group of like-minded women to connect with in community, prayer, and study. What I found, though I didn't know it at the time, was the beginning of a process that would transform me from student to teacher, leaving me lying awake in my bed at night plotting how to get more spoons into the hands of more women, praying that many mountains might be thrown into the sea.

This book intends to equip you with the best spoon I can offer. It intends to teach you not merely a doctrine, concept, or story line, but a study method that will allow you to open up the Bible on your own. It intends to challenge you to think and to grow, using tools accessible to all of us, whether we hold a high school diploma or a seminary degree, whether we have minutes or hours to give to it each day. This book intends to change the way you think about Bible study.

Perhaps your story is not like mine at all—perhaps you have spent your entire life in the same church or in no church at all. My guess is that you know the dim discomfort of living in the shadow of a mountain.

It has been said that we become what we behold. I believe there is nothing more transformative to our lives than beholding God in his Word. After all, how can we conform to the image of a God we have not beheld? On the other side of the mountain of my biblical ignorance was a vision of God high and lifted up, a vision stretching from Genesis to Revelation that I desperately needed to see. I have by no means removed that whole mountain from my line of sight, but I intend to go to my grave with dirt beneath my nails and a spoon clutched in my fist. I am determined that no mountain of biblical ignorance will keep me from seeing him as clearly as my seventy or eighty years on this earth will allow.

So this is a book for those who are ready to start digging. This is a book for those who are ready to face squarely the mountain of their fragmented understanding of Scripture, and brandishing a spoon, command it to move.

1

Turning Things Around

> All Scripture is breathed out by God and profitable for teaching, for reproof, for correction, and for training in righteousness, that the man of God may be complete, equipped for every good work.
>
> 2 Tim. 3:16–17

This is a book about equipping women through Bible study. Outside of my family, it's the thing I care most about. But this hasn't always been the case. Long before I had a passion for teaching the Bible, I had a deep and abiding passion for something else. Four-year-old-me had a passion for rhumba tights.

You remember rhumba tights—those tights for little girls made extra fancy by four rows of ruffled lace sewn across the seat? I absolutely loved them. I wore dresses to preschool every day so I could wear my special tights. When I ran out of dresses, undeterred, I crammed those tights under my jeans. Bulky? Yes. Uncomfortable? Absolutely. Beautiful? You know it.

I loved everything about them, except for one thing—the ruffles were in the back where the wearer could not enjoy seeing them. All that beautiful lace out of eyesight? Unacceptable. But a simple solution presented itself: I began wearing them backwards.

Problem solved. Until my mother caught on.

I don't know if it was the heel section of the foot flopping out the top of my Mary Janes or the way my stomach bulged suspiciously beneath my skirt. Maybe it was the funny way I had to walk to keep them from falling down, or my frequent habit of twirling in front of mirrors. Let's just say that wearing my rhumba tights backwards presented some coverage issues that wearing them correctly did not. My mother informed me that improper usage was not an option. Rhumba tights were made to be worn a particular way for a particular purpose, and I either needed to turn them around or give up the privilege of those four glorious rows of lace.

I wish I could say this was the only time in my life I got something backwards. It wasn't. In fact, my passion for teaching women the Bible is actually the result of getting other things backwards as well. I want to tell you about two approaches I took to being equipped by Scripture that seemed right at the outset but were completely backwards.

It might seem that studying the Bible would be something we should know how to do intuitively. After all, if God discloses his will and character there, wouldn't the Holy Spirit just open up its message to our hearts? But this is not the case. Yes, the Holy Spirit opens the Word to us, but not without some effort on our part.

Do you know that the word *disciple* means "learner"? As a disciple of Christ, you and I are called to learn, and learning requires effort. It also requires good study methods. We know this to be true of our schooling, but do we know it to be true of following Christ? Though I was a good student in school, I was not always a good student of the Word, and left to my own devices I probably would not have become one. But through the faithful teaching of others, my tendency to get a good thing backwards came to light. Turning around my two backwards approaches to Bible study started me toward a lifelong love of learning, applying, and teaching.

Turnaround 1: Let the Bible Speak of God

The first thing I got backwards seems so obviously backwards that it's embarrassing to admit: I failed to understand that the Bible is a book about God. The Bible is a book that boldly and clearly reveals who God is on every page. In Genesis, it does this by placing God as the subject of the creation narrative. In Exodus, it places him in comparison to Pharaoh and the gods of Egypt. In the Psalms, David extols the Lord's power and majesty. The prophets proclaim his wrath and justice. The Gospels and Epistles unfold his character in the person and work of Christ. The book of Revelation displays his dominion over all things. From beginning to end, the Bible is a book about God.

Perhaps I really did know that the Bible was a book about God, but I didn't realize that I wasn't reading it as if it were.

This is where I got things backwards: I approached my study time asking the wrong questions. I read the Bible asking, "Who am I?" and "What should I do?" And the Bible did answer these questions in places. Ephesians 2:10 told me that I was God's workmanship. The Sermon on the Mount told me to ask for daily bread and to store up treasure in heaven. The story of King David told me to seek after the heart of God. But the questions I was asking revealed that I held a subtle misunderstanding about the very nature of the Bible: I believed that the Bible was a book about me.

I believed that I should read the Bible to teach me how to live and to assure me that I was loved and forgiven. I believed it was a roadmap for life, and that in any given circumstance, someone who truly knew how to read and interpret it could find a passage to give comfort or guidance. I believed the purpose of the Bible was to help me.

In this belief, I was not so different from Moses standing before the burning bush on Mount Sinai. Immediately within his view was a revelation of the character of God: a bush in flames, speaking audibly to him, miraculously not consumed. When charged by this vision of God to go to Pharaoh and demand release of the captives, Moses self-consciously replies, "*Who am I* that I should go to Pharaoh and bring the children of Israel out of Egypt?" (Ex. 3:11).

God responds by patiently making himself the subject of the narrative: "But I will be with you" (Ex. 3:12). Rather than be reassured by this answer, Moses next asks, "What should *I* do?": "Then Moses said to God, 'If *I* come to the people of Israel and say to them, "The God of your fathers has sent me to you," and they ask me, "What is his name?" what shall *I* say to them?'" (v. 13).

Notice that rather than telling Moses what he should do, God instead tells him what *he* has done, is doing, and will do:

> God said to Moses, "*I am who I am*." And he said, "Say this to the people of Israel, '*I am* has sent me to you.'" God also said to Moses, "Say this to the people of Israel, '*The Lord, the God of your fathers, the God of Abraham, the God of Isaac, and the God of Jacob*, has sent me to you.' This is my name forever, and thus *I am* to be remembered throughout all generations. Go and gather the elders of Israel together and say to them, '*The Lord, the God of your fathers, the God of Abraham, of Isaac, and of Jacob*, has appeared to me, saying, "*I have* observed you and what has been done to you in Egypt, and *I promise* that *I will* bring you up out of the affliction of Egypt. . . ."' And they will listen to your voice, and you and the elders of Israel shall go to the king of Egypt and say to him, '*The Lord, the God of the Hebrews*, has met with us; and now, please let us go a three days' journey into the wilderness, that we may sacrifice to the Lord our God.' But *I know* that the king of Egypt will not let you go unless compelled by a mighty hand. So *I will* stretch out my hand and strike Egypt with all the wonders that *I will* do in it; after that he will let you go. And *I will* give this people favor in the sight of the Egyptians; and when you go, you shall not go empty." (Ex. 3:14–22)

The dialogue continues in this manner. For an entire chapter and a half of Exodus, Moses asks the wrong questions: Who am I? What should I do? Rather than answer him, "Moses, you are my chosen servant. You are my precious creation, a gifted and wise leader," God responds by completely removing Moses from the subject of the discussion and inserting himself. He answers Moses's self-focused question of "Who am I?" with the only answer that matters: "I AM."

We are like Moses. The Bible is our burning bush—a faithful declaration of the presence and holiness of God. We ask it to tell us about ourselves, and all the while it is telling us about "I AM." We think that if it would just tell us who we are and what we should do, then our insecurities, fears, and doubts would vanish. But our insecurities, fears, and doubts can never be banished by the knowledge of who we are. They can only be banished by the knowledge of "I AM." We must read and study the Bible with our ears trained on hearing God's declaration of himself.

Does this mean that the Bible has nothing to say to us about who we are? Not at all. We just go about trying to answer that question in a backwards way. The Bible does tell us who we are and what we should do, but it does so through the lens of who God is. The knowledge of God and the knowledge of self always go hand in hand. In fact, there can be no true knowledge of self apart from the knowledge of God. He is the only reference point that is reliable. So, when I read that God is longsuffering, I realize that I am not longsuffering. When I read that God is slow to anger, I realize that I am quick to anger. When I read that God is just, I realize that I am unjust. Seeing who he is shows me who I am in a true light. A vision of God high and lifted up reveals to me my sin and increases my love for him. Grief and love lead to genuine repentance, and I begin to be conformed to the image of the One I behold.

If I read the Bible looking for myself in the text before I look for God there, I may indeed learn that I should not be selfish. I may even try harder not to be selfish. But until I see my selfishness through the lens of the utter unselfishness of God, I have not properly understood its sinfulness. The Bible is a book about God. As Moses would learn during the Exodus, *who he was* bore no impact on the outcome of his situation. *Who God was* made all the difference.

In the New Testament we find Jesus addressing the same problem with the Jewish leaders: "You search the Scriptures because you think that in them you have eternal life; and it is they that *bear witness about me*, yet you refuse to come to me that you may have life" (John 5:39–40). The Jewish leaders searched the Scriptures asking the wrong question, looking for the wrong image to be revealed.

If eternal life is found in the Scriptures, it is found through the lens of who God is. If our reading of the Bible focuses our eyes on anyone other than God, we have gotten backwards the transformation process. Any study of the Bible that seeks to establish our identity without first proclaiming God's identity will render partial and limited help. We must turn around our habit of asking "Who am I?" We must first ask, "What does this passage teach me about God?" before we ask it to teach us anything about ourselves. We must acknowledge that the Bible is a book about God.

Turnaround 2: Let the Mind Transform the Heart

The second thing I got backwards in my approach to the Bible was the belief that my heart should guide my study. The heart, as it is spoken of in Scripture, is the seat of the will and emotions. It is our "feeler" and our "decision-maker." Letting my heart guide my study meant that I looked for the Bible to make me feel a certain way when I read it. I wanted it to give me peace, comfort, or hope. I wanted it to make me feel closer to God. I wanted it to give me assurance about tough choices. Because I wanted the Bible to engage my emotions, I spent little time in books like Leviticus or Numbers and much time in books like the Psalms and the Gospels.

The Bible commands us to love God with all of our hearts (Mark 12:30). When we say that we love God with all of our hearts, we mean that we love him completely with our emotions and with our wills. Attaching our emotions to our faith comes fairly naturally for women—generally speaking, we know how to be emotive without much guidance. If we think of the heart as the seat of our emotions and our will, it makes sense that we so often approach God's Word asking, "Who am I?" and "What should I do?" Those two questions uniquely address the heart. And we speak often in the church about how Christianity is a religion of the heart—of how Christ comes into our hearts, of how we need heart-change. It is right to speak of Christianity in this way, but not exclusively in this way.

Interestingly, the same verse that commands us to love God with all of our hearts also commands us to love him with all of our minds. Our minds are the seat of our intellects. Attaching our intellect to our faith does not come naturally to most of us. We live in a time when faith and reason are spoken of as polar opposites. At times, the church has even embraced this kind of language. For some of us, the strength of our faith is gauged by how close we feel to God at any given moment—by how a sermon made us feel, by how a worship chorus made us feel, by how our quiet time made us feel. Hidden in this thinking is an honest desire to share a deep relationship with a personal God, but sustaining our emotions can be exhausting and defeating. Changing circumstances can topple our emotional stability in an instant. Our "walk with the Lord" can feel more like a roller-coaster ride of peaks and valleys than a straight path in which valleys and mountains have been made level.

Could this be because we've gotten things backwards? By asking our hearts to lead our minds, have we willingly purchased a ticket to the roller-coaster ride? Unless we turn things around, placing the mind in charge of the heart, we could be in for a long, wild ride.

Asking us to put our minds before our hearts sounds almost unspiritual, doesn't it? But notice the way that Scripture talks about the role of the mind:

> *In repentance:* "If they *repent with all their mind* and with all their heart in the land of their enemies . . . then hear in heaven your dwelling place their prayer and their plea. . . ." (1 Kings 8:48–49)

> *In seeking God:* "Now *set your mind* and heart to seek the LORD your God." (1 Chron. 22:19)

In finding peace: "You keep him in perfect peace *whose mind is stayed* on you, because he trusts in you." (Isa. 26:3)

In right worship: "For if I pray in a tongue, my spirit prays but *my mind is unfruitful*. What am I to do? I will pray with my spirit, but I will *pray with my mind* also; I will sing praise with my spirit, but I will *sing with my mind* also." (1 Cor. 14:14–15)

In understanding the Scriptures: "Then [Jesus] said to [the disciples], 'These are my words that I spoke to you while I was still with you, that everything written about me in the Law of Moses and the Prophets and the Psalms must be fulfilled.' Then *he opened their minds to understand the Scriptures*." (Luke 24:44–45)

In transforming us: "Do not be conformed to this world, but be *transformed by the renewal of your mind*, that by testing you may discern what is the will of God, what is good and acceptable and perfect." (Rom. 12:2–3)

Don't rush past that pivotal truth you just read in Romans 12:2–3. What Christian doesn't desperately want life transformation and knowledge of the will of God? In these verses, Paul states unequivocally how we can have them: by the renewing of *our minds—not our hearts*.

For years I tried to love God with my heart to the neglect of my mind, not recognizing my need to grow in the knowledge of the "I AM." Any systematic study of the Bible felt mechanical, even a little like an act of faithlessness or an admission that the Holy Spirit's insight during a quiet time wasn't enough for me. But I was missing the important truth that *the heart cannot love what the mind does not know.* This is the message of Romans 12:2–3—not that the mind alone affects transformation, but that the path to transformation runs from the mind to the heart, and not the other way around.

The scientific community has noted this mind-before-heart connection. Paul Bloom, a Yale professor with a PhD in cognitive psychology, specializes in pleasure research—the study of how we as humans develop the ability to derive pleasure from people, experiences, and things. He has discovered through his research that pleasure does not simply occur, it develops. And how it develops is a point worth noting: "People ask me, 'How do you get more pleasure out of life?' And my answer is extremely pedantic: Study more. . . . The key to enjoying wine isn't just to guzzle a lot of expensive wine, it's to learn about wine."[1]

Bloom has found that pleasure results from gaining knowledge about the object of our pleasure, not, as we might assume, from merely experiencing it over and over. Specifically, our pleasure increases in something when we learn its history, origin, and deeper nature.[2] This is particularly relevant to Christians. We are called to be a people who delight ourselves in the Lord, who can say with conviction that "at your right hand are pleasures forevermore" (Ps. 16:11) Many of us identify readily with the call to Christian hedonism. Yet we fight daily to live as those whose greatest pleasure is found in God. If Bloom is right, finding greater pleasure in God will not result from pursuing more experiences of him, but from knowing him better. It will result from making a study of the Godhead.

Think about the relationship, possession, or interest you derive the most pleasure from. How did you develop that delight? Whether you are passionate about modern art, your car, conservation, your spouse, nutrition, education, or baseball, my guess is that you became that way by learning about the object of your passion—and that your pleasure in it grew as your knowledge grew.

Marriage may be the most obvious example of this process. Most people get married on very little information. Have you noticed this? We stake our future on a relatively short acquaintance, in large part due to a rush of emotion that hits us during the courtship phase. We marry, awash with feelings of love for our spouse, but knowing rather little about him in the grand scheme of things. Those initial feelings of love either dwindle or deepen, depending on how we nurture them. Looking back on twenty years of marriage, I can honestly say that I love my husband exponentially more than I did on our wedding day. Why? Because I have made a study of him, and he of me. Knowing him has grown my love for him. On our wedding day I suspected he would be a good father, a hard worker, and a faithful sounding board, but twenty years later I know him to be these things. My love for him has grown as my knowledge of him has increased.

Now think about your relationship to God in the same light. Most people come to faith in God on very little information. We understand that we need forgiveness and grace, and we're ushered into the kingdom on a wave of deep emotion. But we hold only a small sense of the One who has brought us to himself. We suspect that he is all good things, but we have not yet made a study of him. Like a new bride, we reach the end of the honeymoon phase and begin to wonder how we are to sustain and nurture this relationship.

The answer lies in knowing God, in loving him with our minds. Never has the phrase "to know him is to love him" been more true. As we grow in the knowledge of God's character through the study of his Word, we cannot help but grow into an exponentially deeper love for him. This explains why Romans 12:2 says we are transformed by the renewing of our minds. We come to understand who God is, and we are changed—our affections detach from lesser things and attach to him. If we want to feel a deeper love for God, we must learn to see him more clearly for who he is. If we want to feel deeply about God, we must learn to think deeply about God.

Consider another illustration: If I told you that I loved the piano and took great enjoyment in playing it, how could you discover whether my feelings about the piano were real or not? Simple. Just ask me to play for you. A person who truly loves to play the piano disciplines herself to make a study of it. Through much application of mental discipline, her proficiency at playing—and consequently, her love for playing—grow and flourish.

The heart cannot love what the mind does not know. Yes, it is sinful to acquire knowledge for knowledge's sake, but acquiring knowledge about One we love, for the sake of loving him more deeply, will always be for our transformation.

We must love God with our minds, allowing our intellect to inform our emotions, rather than the other way around.

God before Me, Mind before Heart

Seeing ourselves in the Bible and engaging our emotions in loving God are beautiful things. They are the metaphorical ruffles on the rhumba tights of Bible study. But they belong in the back, a secondary reward for obediently seeking that which is primary. Bible study that equips does not neglect self-knowledge, but it puts self-knowledge in the right place: informed by the knowledge of God. Bible study that equips does not divorce the heart from study, but it puts the heart in the right place: informed by the mind.

Perhaps you have gotten things backwards like me. Perhaps you've realized the ill-fitting discomfort of Bible study that focuses on who you are and what you should do more than on who God is, or of Bible study that targets your emotions more than your intellect. It's not too late to turn things around. Let's move forward, asking the Lord to show us a "ruffles in back" approach to learning the Bible.

2

The Case for Bible Literacy

> For whatever was written in former days was written for our instruction, that through endurance and through the encouragement of the Scriptures we might have hope.
>
> Rom. 15:4

A little heads-up: this is the chapter you don't want to read. This is the chapter where you get uncomfortable and want to tell me to mind my own business. This is the chapter where we talk about Bible literacy: what it is, whether we are acquiring it, and why it matters that we do so.

Let me put you at ease: most of us don't have it, myself included. Bible literacy is something most of us will never feel comfortable claiming we have achieved during our lifetime. So this is a chapter that makes me uncomfortable, too.

We all carry around the dim discomfort of our not-knowing, feeling it surge to the surface when we enter into conversations with the unbeliever, the friend in our small group, the wise older woman. Sometimes when a category on Jeopardy covers a Bible topic, we experience a moment of sheer panic that Alex Trebek knows his way around our sacred text better than we do. We would be hard-pressed to name the twelve apostles or to give the order of the creation story. We have heard of Tamar, but was she a positive example or a negative one? When two preachers we love take differing positions on the same passage, we are thrown into confusion.

We treasure what we know, but we are troubled by what we do not know. We do our best to cobble together a patchwork knowledge of Scripture, pieced from sermons, studies, and quiet times, but we are often confronted with the gaps and loose seams in the garment of our understanding, particularly when life gets hard. We don't know our Bibles like we need to—some of us who are new to the faith don't know them at all, and many of us who have been in the church for decades are scarcely better off.

But what can we do to know the Bible better? We have already begun to answer the question of what makes for sound Bible study: sound Bible study transforms the heart by training the mind and it places God at the center of the story. But sound Bible study does more than that—it leaves the student with a better understanding of the Bible than she had when she started. Stated another way, sound Bible study increases Bible literacy.

What Is Bible Literacy?

Bible literacy occurs when a person has access to a Bible in a language she understands and is steadily moving toward knowledge and understanding of the text. If it is true that the character and will of God are proclaimed in Scripture, then any serious attempt to become equipped for the work of discipleship must include a desire to build Bible literacy. Bible literacy stitches patchwork knowledge into a seamless garment of understanding.

If you are reading this book, then you probably have access to a Bible in a language you understand. This is no small gift. What you need is steady movement toward knowledge and understanding. This steady movement does not occur by accident, nor does it always occur intuitively. We may have an earnest desire to build Bible literacy, but left untrained, we may develop habits of engaging the text that at best do nothing to increase literacy and at worst actually work against it. Before we can develop good habits, we must take an honest inventory of the unhelpful ones we may already practice.

Have you ever had an unhelpful habit that you wanted to break? In my early twenties I realized I had an unhelpful habit of completing other peoples' sentences. I remember how surprised I was when someone lovingly pointed out to me that I shouldn't do that. It wasn't that I didn't know I completed other people's sentences—it was that I didn't see anything wrong with it. I actually believed I was helping the conversation along by jumping in. But once I became aware that I was doing it, I realized how often it was happening and how disrespectful it was to others. I was embarrassed and ashamed, and I was filled with an immediate desire to stop. But by the time I realized the problem, I had formed a well-established pattern of communication that was difficult to break. Learning to stop my unhelpful habit required recognizing the extent of my problem and then working hard to change the pattern.

This is true of any unhelpful habit we might develop, especially if the habit has developed over the course of years. In order to break it, we must first recognize the extent of its influence and then take steps to change.

When it comes to studying the Bible, unhelpful habits abound. Within our Christian subculture we have adopted a catch-all phrase for our regular habit of interacting with Scripture: "spending time in the Word." Church leaders urge us to do so. Authors and bloggers exhort us to value it. But what should take place during our "time in the Word" can remain a vague notion, the specific habits it represents varying widely from person to person.

The potential danger of this vagueness is that we may assume that our version of "spending time in the Word" is moving us toward Bible literacy simply because we have been obedient to practice it. Not all contact with Scripture builds Bible literacy. Learning what the Bible says and subsequently working to interpret and apply it requires quite a different practice than many of those we commonly associate with "spending time in the Word." We cannot afford to assume that our good intentions are enough.

Are We Growing in Bible Literacy?

If Bible literacy is to be our goal, we need an honest evaluation of what we are currently doing to achieve it. Some of our existing habits may not be "bad" in the sense that they accomplish nothing to help us learn God's Word—they may simply be limiting, in the sense that they can only take us so far in our understanding. Other habits probably need to be put aside completely. At first we may not be able to perceive that our current approaches are limiting or unhelpful, but on closer examination we begin to notice the gaps in understanding that they can leave.

In my years of teaching women the Bible, I have come across several common unhelpful habits of "spending time in the Word." I wonder if any of them will sound familiar to you.

The Xanax Approach

Feel anxious? Philippians 4:6 says be anxious for nothing. Feel ugly? Psalm 139 says you are fearfully and wonderfully made. Feel tired? Matthew 11:28 says Jesus will give rest to the weary. The Xanax Approach treats the Bible as if it exists to make us feel better. Whether aided by a devotional book or just the topical index in my Bible, I pronounce my time in the Word successful if I can say, "Wow. That was really comforting."

The Problem: The Xanax Approach makes the Bible a book about me. I ask how the Bible can serve me, rather than how I can serve the God it proclaims. In reality, the Bible doesn't always make us feel better. In fact, quite often it does just the opposite. (Feeling awesome? Jeremiah 17:9 says we're wicked rascals.) Yes, there is comfort to be found in the pages of Scripture, but context is what makes that comfort lasting and real. Note also that the Xanax Approach guarantees that huge sections of our Bibles will remain unread because they fail to deliver an immediate dose of emotional satisfaction. We are not very likely to read Leviticus or Lamentations if we subscribe to this approach. A well-rounded approach to Bible study challenges us to navigate all areas of the Bible, even those that make us uncomfortable or that are difficult to understand.

The Pinball Approach

Lacking a preference or any guidance about what to read, I read whatever Scripture I happen to turn to. Hey, it's all good, right? I'll just ask the Holy Spirit to speak to me through whatever verse I flip to. Releasing the plunger of my good intentions, I send the pinball of my ignorance hurtling toward whatever passage it may hit, ricocheting around to various passages "as the Spirit leads."

The Problem: The Bible was not written to be read this way. The Pinball Approach gives no thought to cultural, historical, or textual context, authorship, or original intent of the passage in question. It does nothing to help us gain understanding of the text beyond our immediate context. When we read this way, we treat the Bible with less respect than we would give to a simple textbook. Imagine trying to master algebra by randomly reading for ten minutes each day from whatever paragraph in the textbook your eyes happened to fall on. Like that metal pinball, you'd lose momentum fast (and be very bad at algebra). A well-rounded approach to Bible study takes into account how any given passage fits into the bigger picture of what the Bible has to say, honoring context, authorship, style, and more.

The Magic 8 Ball Approach

Remember the Magic 8 Ball? It could answer even our most difficult questions as a child. But I'm an adult now, and I'm wondering if I should marry Bob, get a new job, or change my hair color. I give my Bible a vigorous shake and open it. Placing my finger blindly on a verse, I then read it to see if "signs point to yes."

The Problem: The Bible is not magical and it does not serve our whims, nor is its primary function to answer our questions. The Magic 8 Ball Approach misconstrues the ministry of the Holy Spirit through the Word, demanding that the Bible tell us *what to do* rather than *who to be*. And it's dangerously close to soothsaying, which people used to get stoned for. So, please. No Magic 8 Ball. A well-rounded approach to Bible study recognizes that the Bible is always more concerned with the decision-maker than with the decision itself. Its aim is to change our hearts so that we desire what God desires, rather than to spoon-feed us answers to every decision in life.

The Personal Shopper Approach (a.k.a. the Topical Bible Study)

I want to know about being a godly woman or how to deal with self-esteem issues, but I don't know where to find verses about that, so I let [insert famous Bible teacher here] do the legwork for me. She winsomely hand-selects relevant verses from all over the Bible and delivers them to my doorstep to be tried on for size.

The Problem: The Personal Shopper Approach doesn't help us build "ownership" of Scripture. Much like the Pinball Approach, we ricochet from passage to passage, gaining fragmentary knowledge of many books of the Bible but mastery of none. Topical studies do hold potential to help us grow, but we risk something by calling them "Bible studies." Calling a book on body image a Bible study implies that it is teaching us a working knowledge of Scripture. Many topical studies, even good ones, cannot fairly make this claim. They offer value as a supplement to—but not a substitute for—studying the Bible in its most basic sense. Topical studies serve a purpose: they help us integrate broad concepts into our understanding of Scripture. But they are not foundational. If they are all we ever do, we will miss out on the richness of learning a book of the Bible from start to finish. A well-rounded approach to Bible study addresses a topic as it arises in Scripture, rather than attaching Scripture to a topic. It asks the student to labor at the process of discovery.

The Telephone Game Approach

Remember playing the telephone game? Where you sat in a circle and whispered a sentence into the ear of the person next to you? The fun lay in seeing how garbled the message was by the time it made it around the circle. A similar process can happen when we read books *about* the Bible instead of reading the Bible itself. Why? Because authors build on the writings of others. This isn't wrong—it's actually logical. But it's something a student should be aware of. If I prefer reading what others have written about the Bible to reading the Bible itself, I am probably reading what someone says about what someone says about what the Bible says. As with topical studies, books about the Bible can be helpful, but they are not foundational. If I can quote John Piper more than I can quote the apostle Paul, I've probably been practicing the Telephone Game Approach. Sometimes without even noticing it, I can slip into this pattern. This is because books about the Bible don't require as much work to understand as the Bible itself, and they are usually written by people who seem to know way more about the Bible than I ever will.

The Problem: We're called to love the Lord our God with all of *our* mind, not John Piper's mind. While what he and others have to say about the Bible can be extremely helpful, it is no substitute for Bible study on our own. Why would we spend more time reading a text several times removed from Scripture than we spend reading Scripture itself? We'll get way more out of Piper if we invest our time in the book he loves above all others. A well-rounded approach to Bible study recognizes that books about the Bible, like topical studies, are a supplement to personal study, not a substitute for it. Unless we are growing in Bible literacy, their ability to help us will be limited. The more we grow in Bible literacy, the more helpful supplements and commentaries become.

The Jack Sprat Approach

I take this approach when I engage in "picky eating" with the Word of God. I read the New Testament, but other than Psalms and Proverbs, I avoid the Old Testament, or I read books with characters, plots, or topics I can easily identify with. Women, in particular, seem drawn to this approach (anyone else a little worn out with Esther, Ruth, and Proverbs 31?), but everyone fights this temptation to a certain extent.

The Problem: All Scripture is God-breathed and profitable. All of it. We need a balanced diet to grow to maturity—it's time to move on to the rest of the meal. Women need both male and female examples to point us to godliness. We can't fully appreciate the sweetness of the New Testament without the savory of the Old Testament. We need historical narrative, poetry, wisdom literature, law, prophecy, and parables all showing us the character of God from different angles. And we need to see the gospel story from Genesis to Revelation. A well-rounded approach to Bible study challenges us to learn the full counsel of God's Word. It helps us to build a collective understanding of how the Bible as a whole speaks of God.

* * *

Did you see anything familiar in these six approaches? Recognizing an unhelpful habit is never fun, but it marks the beginning of making a change for the better. I can vouch for having practiced all of these at one time or another on the road to discovering a better approach. I admit that hearing so many other women report having used the same approaches was a little bit of a relief, but it was also frustrating to learn that so many of us appear to be in the same boat. If we have never been trained how to be a good student of the Bible, it is no surprise that we have looked for ways to improvise. If anything, the prevalence of these practices probably reveals a blind spot in the church's vision for discipling, rather than a lack of willingness to learn on the part of the disciple.

Breaking existing habits is hard work, and only those who believe the end result will be worth the effort will put in the work to break them. We must recognize that a better way beckons to us. We must combine our willingness to learn with an approach that will build Bible literacy. We must learn to study in such a way that we are not just absorbing the insights of another, but are actually being equipped to interpret and apply Scripture on our own. Every study we undertake should do more than just teach us a book of the Bible; it should teach us how to study any book of the Bible with greater effectiveness.

Why Bible Literacy Matters

Do you believe in the importance of reclaiming Bible literacy? Let me suggest a reason why you should: Bible literacy matters because it protects us from falling into error. Both the false teacher and the secular humanist rely on biblical ignorance for their messages to take root, and the modern church has proven fertile ground for those messages. Because we do not know our Bibles, we crumble at the most basic challenges to our worldview. Disillusionment and apathy eat away at our ranks. Women, in particular, are leaving the church in unprecedented numbers.[1]

When women grow increasingly lax in their pursuit of Bible literacy, everyone in their circle of influence is affected. Rather than acting as salt and light, we become bland contributions to the environments we inhabit and shape, indistinguishable from those who have never been changed by the gospel. Home, church, community, and country desperately need the influence of women who know why they believe what they believe, grounded in the Word of God. They desperately need the influence of women who love deeply and actively the God proclaimed in the Bible.

Maybe you have felt your own interest in the Bible waning and have wondered why. You may have even questioned your love of God in light of your lack of desire to know his Word. I believe that a woman who loses interest in her Bible has not been equipped to love it as she should. The God of the Bible is too lovely to abandon for lesser pursuits. I want women everywhere to develop a deep and abiding love for him through the study of the text that makes him known.

In the following chapters, I want to show you how. Like many teachers, I have a soft spot for alliteration, so grant me your tolerance as we explore how to value what I call the Five P's of Sound Study:

Study with **Purpose**
Study with **Perspective**
Study with **Patience**
Study with **Process**
Study with **Prayer**

As we move through our Five P's of Sound Study, you will no doubt begin to notice that their relationship to one another is not strictly linear. We will build on each idea as we address it, but the order in which we will discuss them does not communicate that one is more important than another. We will consider the importance of *prayer* last, though it is certainly not of last importance in our approach to Scripture, nor is it the last element we should practice. Each of the Five P's supports the others: we *pray* for *patience* to study well. *Perspective* and *process* are intertwined and rely on keeping *purpose* in view. Bearing in mind that all five *P's* are equally necessary and interrelated, we will organize our discussion of them by moving in an order from general to specific.

Each of these vantage points will help us begin to grow in Bible literacy, training us in the exercise of mind-before-heart, God-before-self. So let's get started.

3

Study with Purpose

> Do you not know? Do you not hear? Has it not been told you from the beginning? Have you not understood from the foundations of the earth? It is he who sits above the circle of the earth.
>
> Isa. 40:21–22a

When I was a little girl, my father used to take my brothers and me on camping trips. At first I believed that we took these trips because my father loved the outdoors. As I grew older, I began to realize that what my father loved more than anything was a comfortable bed, a solid roof over his head, and predictable access to the evening news on a TV set. I strove to make sense of these facts as they related to camping. Why on earth had we spent weekends out in the elements eating out of tin cans when my father was so clearly not a lover of outdoor adventures? When I became a parent myself, the reason became clear: He had not taken us camping because he loved camping; he had taken us camping because he loved *us*. As his purpose became clear to me, his willingness to forgo creature comforts for mosquito repellent and tent pegs also began to make perfect sense.

Every good endeavor should be done with purpose. Without a clear sense of purpose, our efforts to do a good thing well can flounder. But with a clear purpose, we are far more likely to persevere. This is certainly true of building Bible literacy—it takes effort to build, but maintaining a clear sense of purpose sustains us in our labor. How can we begin to be more purposeful in the way we approach Bible study?

It might seem terribly obvious to say that we should study the Bible with purpose. Certainly, we all have some purpose in mind when we begin to study—we noted a few of them in the previous chapter: to make us feel a certain way, to help us make decisions, to help us with self-discovery. But we want to have in mind the purpose that the Bible itself intends us to have when we open its cover. No lesser purpose will do.

We have already considered that the Bible is a book about God, but now let's consider that truth in more specific terms. From Genesis to Revelation, the Bible is telling us about the reign and rule of God. This is the Big Story of the Bible, the purpose for which it was written. Each of its sixty-six books contributes to telling this Big Story—a story of creation, fall, redemption, and restoration. The Bible purposes to tell us this Big Story in a thousand smaller stories, from its first page to its last.

It follows, then, that our purpose in studying must be to look for that Big Story each time we go to the Scriptures. We should study asking not just what a particular portion of Scripture wants to tell us, but how that portion of Scripture is telling us the Big Story of the Bible as a whole. Studying the Bible with purpose means keeping its overarching message in view at all times, whether we are in the Old Testament or the New, whether we are in the Minor Prophets or the Gospels. In order to do this, we must "zoom out" from any one particular book or passage and gain an appreciation for how it plays its part in unfolding the Big Story.

What a Plane Ticket Taught Me

I gained a clearer understanding of this Big Story principle on a vacation. Most vacations find our family making the ten-hour drive from Dallas, Texas, to Santa Fe, New Mexico, to spend time with grandparents. We have grown accustomed to the trip—coffee stop in Wichita Falls, lunch in Amarillo, snack in Tucumcari. The scenery on the drive is intermittently spectacular, and the kids know exactly where I will tell them to drop whatever they are doing to enjoy a mandatory "nature moment." My husband is a lover of maps, and his faithful recitation of the topographical changes to the landscape is always a hit:

"We're on the southern plains now . . ."

"Just entered the Red River Valley . . ."

"Here we go up onto the Llano Estacado . . ."

"We're dropping into the Mesalands . . ."

The fact that he even knows these details has always been a marvel to me. His high school geography teacher should be basking in the glow of a job well done. And mine should be languishing in obscurity: I haven't known the topography because I was never taught the topography.

So it wasn't until I had a reason to fly out to Santa Fe that I began to fully appreciate what my husband knew. As we lifted off and turned west, I suddenly realized I was watching the southern plains unfurl beneath me, transected by the Red River Valley, punctuated by the Llano Estacado. I saw the fingers of the Mesalands reaching toward the mountains in the north. I saw from a bird's-eye view the story I had only appreciated in part, and suddenly all the intermittently spectacular moments of the drive fit together into one continuous and stunning landscape. The perspective I gained on that flight forever changed the way I perceived the drive. For the price of a plane ticket, my children gained not one, but two parents babbling about topography for ten hours each holiday.

The Big Story of the Bible

The Bible has its own topography, its own set of "geographical features" that fit together to form one continuous and stunning landscape. But many of us have never bought the plane ticket to understand its contours. Many of us, after years in the church, don't know the topography because we haven't been taught the topography. We know when we are seeing something beautiful in the pages of Scripture, but we don't always know how what we are seeing fits with the rest of the story. Our understanding of Scripture is a fragmented series of "nature moments" that may move us deeply but do not necessarily connect together to reveal the bigger picture.

But without the bigger picture, we can gain only a partial appreciation of what any individual snapshot is trying to tell us. From Genesis to Revelation the Bible is telling us about the reign and rule of God. Its topography speaks of creation, fall, redemption, and restoration in every vista. The topography of the Big Story is populated with different genres of writing—Historical Narrative, Poetry, Wisdom Literature, Law, Prophecy, Parables, Epistles—all conspiring to expand our understanding of the reign and rule of God in different ways.

The idea of a bigger story explaining smaller stories is not unique to the Bible. Scholars call it the *metanarrative*—the comprehensive explanation or guiding theme that illumines all other themes in a text. A metanarrative is essentially a story about stories, encompassing and explaining the "little stories" it overarches. The metanarrative of Margaret Mitchell's *Gone with the Wind* could be described as a story of oppression, transformation, and self-reliance. The novel's big story is told from different angles through the individual stories of the book's characters.

As a gardener, I can't help but think of metanarrative in gardening terms. Just as the Bible's metanarrative is one of creation-fall-redemption-restoration, the gardener's metanarrative is the story of winter, spring, summer, and fall. Every plant and tree in my yard tells its own unique story in flower, fruit, and leaf, but each of those stories points to the bigger story of the passing of the seasons. If I had no understanding of seasons, I might not understand why my tree was suddenly yellow instead of green. I might misinterpret this change to be a sign of disease, rather than an indicator of autumn. Because I understand the metanarrative of gardening, I do not look for tomatoes on my tomato plant in the winter. Nor do I ask my jasmine vine to bloom in the fall. I can interpret my plants' behaviors in light of what season we are in, and I can watch them for signs of what part of the gardening metanarrative is next.

Our disconnect from the metanarrative of the Bible can render us much like a gardener who fails to recognize colored leaves as a sign of autumn rather than a sign of disease. When we are fuzzy about the Big Story, we may have difficulty finding continuity between the God of the Old Testament and the God of the New Testament. We may have trouble relating to the Old Testament at all. We may misinterpret the purpose or emphasis of a smaller story because we have considered it apart from its relationship to the Big Story.

So, consider how the metanarrative of creation-fall-redemption-restoration acts as the Big Story that guides and informs all the small stories. From the window of the airplane, we can look down on the Bible's landscape and note that the *creation* story is introduced in Genesis 1–2: God creates all things for his glory in an orderly manner. He creates man in his image. The *fall* is introduced in Genesis 3: man tries to usurp God's authority, relationship with God is broken, the cosmos is fractured. The theme of *redemption* is introduced immediately in Genesis 3:15, with the promise of salvation coming through Eve. In the rest of Genesis and Exodus, the plan for redemption takes the shape of a people chosen by God—the descendants of Abraham, the nation of Israel. The theme of redemption is explored throughout the rest of the Old Testament from various angles, ultimately pointing toward the perfect redemptive work of Christ on the cross retold to us in the Gospels and explored in the Epistles. The New Testament reinforces and expands our understanding of redemption, assuring us that salvation has been accomplished, urging us to pursue sanctification, and encouraging us to hope in a future glorification. In Revelation, we see the *restoration* of order to the cosmos: God reestablishes perfect order with the creation of a new heaven and new earth.

Knowing how a particular book of the Bible relates to the Big Story is important, but the individual elements of the creation-fall-redemption-restoration theme can also occur in the smaller stories of the Bible, in various combinations. Our task is to search for these themes as we study.

How the Metanarrative Shapes Our Understanding

Consider the story of Noah in Genesis. Many of us have learned the story of Noah and the ark as a heroic tale of a righteous man who built a boat as God commanded, preserving humankind through his obedience. But note how the metanarrative asks us to read the story at a deeper level. Seen in the light of the Big Story, the story of Noah is a story of re-*creation*, in which God returns the earth to its primordial state of disorder and then reorders it just as he did in Genesis 1. He separates water from dry land, restores vegetation, and repopulates his new creation, issuing again the command to be fruitful and multiply. The story of Noah is also a story of *redemption*, in which Noah prefigures Christ. God's faithful servant is willingly shut into an ark (also translated *casket*) by God, passes through the waters of destruction, and is called forth to new life. The story of Noah is also a story of the *fall*. Just when we are ready to proclaim Noah perfect in righteousness, he gets drunk and lies shamefully naked in his tent, reminding us that only one man is perfect in righteousness and able to save us. The story of Noah may hold meaning for us apart from the reference point of the Big Story, but when linked to the Big Story, this smaller story takes on the depth and richness it was intended to have. In relation to the metanarrative, the story of Noah comes into focus as a story about God: God creates, God orders, God preserves life, God provides a deliverer, God alone can save.

Or consider the parable of the Good Samaritan in light of the metanarrative. We often learn this story as a morality tale that challenges us to be kind to others, even when it is inconvenient. But how was Jesus referencing the metanarrative when he crafted this story? The Good Samaritan is a parable that echoes the themes of *fall*, *redemption*, and *restoration*. It is the story of a man rejected by the Jews (the Samaritan) preserving the life of a man who would surely die without his intervention (the man by the road). This Samaritan is under no obligation to intervene, but does so at great personal expense, providing for the helpless man's ongoing care and promising to return to settle accounts. Seen in relation to the metanarrative, the parable of the Good Samaritan is a story about God: God sends the Son to be rejected by his own, to save us from certain death, to restore all things.

Are we called to be like Noah? Yes. Are we called to be like the Good Samaritan? Yes. But not simply because they are positive examples to inspire us to righteousness. These stories point us to Christ. They point us to the Big Story of God's reign and rule, inviting us to see ourselves in relation to him. The knowledge of God and the knowledge of self always go hand in hand: we see the righteousness of Christ illustrated in these two stories, and we respond by crying out for grace to do as God has done for us in Christ: deliver us from the flood of his wrath; rescue us from certain death.

But what about those books or sections of the Bible that are not narrative or storytelling? Law, Poetry, Wisdom Literature, and Prophecy all speak to the metanarrative as well. We will examine how to approach each of these genres in greater detail in chapter 4, but for now, let's consider them briefly (and very generally) in light of the metanarrative of creation-fall-redemption-restoration:

Law: the Bible records God's law for us so that we will understand our need for *redemption* through Christ. It also shows the believer how to obey God by illustrating his character and calling us to be conformed to his image, thereby beginning the process of *restoration* of the image of God that was lost at the *fall*.

Poetry: The poetry of the Bible ranges from laments to blessings to hymns of praise to prophecies. Poetic language and imagery can be used by the authors of Scripture to emphasize or reinforce any part of the metanarrative. The familiar Psalm 23 points to *redemption* and *restoration*. God's well-known response to the questioning of Job (30–40) points to *creation* and *fall*.

Wisdom Literature: As with the Law, Wisdom Literature has a way of showing us the gaps in our sanctification and prompting us to respond in obedience. It, too, points to our need for *redemption* and the ongoing work of *restoration* in the life of the believer.

Prophecy: When we study prophecy, we learn that God does exactly what he says he will do. Seeing the meticulous fulfillment of prophecy in the book of Daniel or Isaiah points us toward the certainty that all as-yet unfulfilled prophecy will also be meticulously fulfilled. Prophecy points to the metanarrative, saying, "*Redemption* has been accomplished, and *restoration* is a certainty."

If only learning to connect a passage of Scripture to the broad vista of the metanarrative were as effortless as buying a plane ticket to Santa Fe. Identifying the metanarrative as we study does not happen effortlessly—it's a study skill that requires time and practice to acquire. All new skills require a learning curve. As you begin to study purposefully—with the Big Story in view—allow yourself a learning curve as your eyes adjust to this new vantage point. Over time, you will become better at integrating individual areas of study into a collective understanding of God's purpose from Genesis to Revelation.

4

Study with Perspective

> Therefore every scribe who has been trained for the kingdom of heaven is like the master of a house, who brings out of his treasure what is new and what is old.
>
> Matt. 13:52

Learning to orient ourselves to the metanarrative of Scripture gives us a clear purpose for our study: to behold the reign and rule of God as revealed in his Word, thereby better understanding our own place in the Big Story. Once we have determined our purpose in these broad terms, we are ready to consider the second *P* of sound study: perspective. We move from asking, "What is the general framework for the Bible as a whole?" to "What is the particular framework for the portion of Scripture I am studying?"

Think again of my road trip to Santa Fe. Amarillo, Texas, is our halfway point, so we usually stop there for a hurried lunch. If you've never been to the Texas Panhandle, let me just say that it isn't exactly a garden spot. Amarillo, in particular, reeks of methane gas for about five miles of freeway because of an ill-placed stockyard. The topography is arid and flat. If Amarillo were a book of the Bible, it would probably correspond to Leviticus: to those just passing through, it's hard to imagine why anyone would want to linger. But if I were to spend time in Amarillo, I would discover that it is a place with its own unique culture and history, a place of cattle ranches, giant wind farms, Palo Duro Canyon, and The Big Texan Steak Ranch (home of the free seventy-two-ounce steak). The more time I spent in Amarillo, the more I might come to appreciate these local treasures. I might never want to leave.

The Bible is much the same way. Not only do all sixty-six books of the Bible tell one sweeping story, but each of those sixty-six books tells its own story, reflecting the character of God through a particular historical and cultural lens. This lens gives us the necessary perspective we need to understand a text correctly. If we take the time to learn the cultural and historical perspective for a book of the Bible, we will better understand how to interpret and value it. But how can we learn to study with the right perspective? To do so, we must become archaeologists.

Unearthing History

The city of Rome has existed since the eighth century BC, a fact its modern-day citizens are keenly aware of. If you own a home in modern-day Rome, history interjects itself into any home improvement project that requires excavation. This is because modern-day Rome is built on top of ancient Rome. Just below the surface of this bustling city lie literally miles of ancient temples, baths, public buildings, and palaces that have vanished from view, many still largely intact.[1] For centuries, Romans have built on top of existing structures, sometimes filling them with dirt to make them a more suitable foundation for new construction. The result is a city upon a city, with here and there the occasional ancient column capital jutting from a modern foundation, hinting at what lies beneath. Archaeologists have meticulously mapped this *Roma subterranea*—"underground Rome"—in an effort to preserve its vanishing record of antiquity, rightly recognizing its value to the modern world.

So when a modern-day Roman homeowner wants to do any renovation requiring digging, almost without exception the archaeologists must be called in.[2] Rome does not allow its residents to dig without regard for its rich and relevant history. All modern-day building must be done with care, recognizing that its current inhabitants live in a context that is much bigger than the short period of time they will dwell there. Living in Rome means paying respect to its original inhabitants, occupying a modern space while maintaining an ancient perspective. The temptation to make one's private residence more livable without notifying the proper agencies would be strong. The desire to say, "Can't I just build to my own liking?" would be great. The past is there for the digging, but only those citizens with a sense of their small place in Rome's history are likely to abide by the city's strict construction codes.

Like the modern-day residents of Rome, modern-day Christians must handle our Bibles with much the same understanding. Modern-day Christians inherit a faith that is built on the foundations of that which has come before. We, too, must occupy a modern space while maintaining an ancient perspective. The earliest portions of our sacred text were written around 1500 BC, in a language we do not speak, to people whose lives looked very different from ours. But many of us choose to build our modern understanding of Scripture with no regard for the historical and cultural context that lies beneath its surface, a context that is essential for a right understanding and application of any text. The temptation to make the Bible applicable to our current experience without preserving its ties to its original audience is strong. The desire to say, "Can't I just read the text as if it were written to me?" is great. The Bible's historical and cultural context is there for the digging, but only those believers with a sense of their small place in redemptive history are likely to dig with diligence.

Digging for Perspective

It is not surprising that the Bible compares the acquisition of wisdom to the finding of gold, silver, and hidden treasure; all three require digging to obtain. And digging is hard work, especially when it must be done with respect to historical and cultural context. We live in a time when the Bible is largely regarded as a book for our own edification, through which the Holy Spirit will simply reveal truth to those willing to give it a few minutes' attention a day. The intellectual muscles that our faith ancestors once used for digging have grown atrophied in the modern mind. Not many of us are willing to do the hard work of digging, preferring to inhabit a modern-day understanding of the Bible with no regard for its original audience or purpose, tailoring our modern reading to suit our own ends. Because we lack a sense of how small we are in the grand scheme of history, we are quick to circumvent the sound practice of "calling in the archaeologists" to help us dig responsibly when we read and study. We need the perspective of the ancients, and that perspective must be excavated.

Scholars call the process of excavating the original meaning of a passage *exegesis*. Each of us is a product of the time and culture in which we live, and as such, we bring certain biases to our reading of Scripture. This is why certain passages can cause us great difficulty the first time we encounter them—passages like, well, basically the entire book of Leviticus. Exegesis pushes on the boundaries of our personal understanding of culture and history, asking us to go back to the time that a text was written and hear it with the ears of its original hearers. Exegesis says, "Before you can hear it with your ears, hear it with theirs. Before you can understand it today, understand it back then." It asks us to take on the perspective of the author and his audience in their original setting. Exegesis asks us to be archaeologists as far as we are able, and to call in the help of more able archaeologists where we need it. It gives us the perspective we need to properly interpret Scripture. It does this by asking five basic archaeological questions of any given text:

1. Who wrote it?
2. When was it written?
3. To whom was it written?
4. In what style was it written?
5. Why was it written?

If you feel like you're back in high school English class right now, that's exactly how I want you to feel. Believe it or not, we do not have to attend seminary to learn how to conduct exegesis of a text. We were probably taught the skills in high school. Part of demystifying Bible study is recognizing that basic principles of literary interpretation are applicable to all books, the Bible included. Much of our difficulty with proper Bible study can be traced to our difficulty with high school English and our hesitation to regard the Bible as literature. Let me assure you of two things:

1. The Bible is in no way diminished by being designated as literature.
2. Your ability to understand the Bible will be greatly enhanced if you treat it as such.

Calling the Bible *literature* is simply acknowledging that it communicates a message through a human author to a human audience in the form of words. According to the dictionary, literature is any written work "having excellence of form or expression and expressing ideas of permanent or universal interest."[3] The Bible is at least that, and much more. But understanding the Bible as literature allows us to employ basic excavation tools that we learned (or should have learned) in school.

Maybe the years have dimmed your memories of high school English, or maybe your class was taught by the football coach. It's not too late to revisit these basic principles of interpretation to help you study the most important piece of literature ever penned. By asking five simple archaeological questions about the text before you begin to read, you can simultaneously fulfill your high school English teacher's dearest hopes and become a better student of your Bible.

Let's briefly address each of these five questions to understand how answering them will impact our study.

1. Who Wrote It?

Most of us would not read a book or an article without considering its source. Knowing who wrote something helps us understand why a text is written one way and not another, and it helps us judge the credibility of what was written. With biblical authors, credibility is not at stake—we come to the text with the assumption that God inspired a particular author to write with full authority. But because we come to the text with this assumption, we sometimes forget to give due consideration to the human element of biblical authorship: God chose a particular person to write a particular book. How does his choice of author influence the way we interpret that book? We do not always know who wrote a particular book of the Bible, but even authorial ambiguity will shape the way we read the text.

Just as knowing that Jefferson, Adams, and Franklin wrote the Declaration of Independence shapes the way we read the document, knowing that Jesus's half brother wrote the book of James shapes the way we read the epistle. We recognize that James wrote as one with firsthand knowledge of Jesus that others would not have had and with a perspective no other writer could claim. We are not surprised to find his writing echo so closely the words of the Sermon on the Mount, and knowing that he died a martyr's death charges us to take seriously his words about living out our faith.

2. When Was It Written?

We use the dating of a book to help us understand how the book would have been read by its original audience, how it speaks uniquely to their moment in history, what other books of the Bible are its contemporaries, and where it fits in the Big Story. Not all books are able to be dated accurately, but many are. In some cases, perhaps most notably the book of Revelation, the date a commentator chooses as most accurate can heavily influence his or her interpretation of the text.

Knowing the approximate date that a book was written helps us to consider the cultural factors that influenced its writing. Combined with our next archaeological question ("To whom was it written?"), dating a book allows us to examine the social structures, gender roles, law codes, geography, and political forces that surrounded the audience to whom the book was originally written. It helps us begin to ask the right questions about an author's underlying assumptions about worship, marriage, family, idolatry, slavery, property ownership, civic duty, and more.

3. To Whom Was It Written?

Every book of the Bible was written to a specific audience who lived in the past. These original hearers lived in times and cultures very different from ours. The message of the Bible transcends its original audience, but it cannot be severed from its original audience. As Gordon Fee and Douglas Stewart note, "A text cannot mean what it never could have meant to its author or his or her readers."[4]

Many of us have been told that "the Bible is God's love letter to us." In one sense, it is, but as we've already considered, first and foremost the Bible is a book about God. When we ask, "To whom was a book written?" we are expanding this first idea to say, "The Bible is a book about God, written to people who lived in the past, and also written to us." Just as we would not study Plato or Socrates without considering their original audience, we cannot study a Bible text without considering its original audience.

Much misapplication of Scripture occurs because modern-day Christians overlook the original audience of a text. Not all promises made to ethnic Israel apply to spiritual Israel (the church). Not all instructions regarding people and property apply to modern culture. We must consider the unique needs, challenges, social structures, and beliefs of those to whom an author originally wrote if we are to appropriately interpret and apply a passage. Before we can ask, "What does this text say to me?" we must ask, "What did this text say to its original audience?"

4. In What Style Was It Written?

In chapter 3 we considered a few of the different literary styles found in Scripture in light of the metanarrative. Each book of the Bible utilizes one or more of these genres to communicate its message. Our ability to accurately interpret and apply a text depends on how well we understand the nuances of each of these genres. Each genre uses language in different ways.

Historical narrative uses language to give a factual retelling of events. It intends to be taken at face value. Knowing this guards us from reading books in this genre as pure myth or allegory. We understand that, first and foremost, the account of the flood should be read as a history. This does not mean that it contains no allegorical elements, but that any allegorical purpose is secondary to the purpose of recounting an actual event.

Parables/storytelling use carefully crafted characters and settings to teach a lesson or illustrate a point. Not every detail of a parable may add significantly to the overall meaning, nor may every character represent someone or something. Characters and settings that may seem odd to us would be easily recognizable to their original audience. Learning to hear these culture-rich stories as their original hearers would have heard them allows us to interpret them properly.

Law codes in the Bible often use language referring to situations or relationships so far removed from our current cultural understanding that we can be at a total loss as to how to understand them. Sometimes the laws recorded are a partial or representative list of a complete body of law that existed elsewhere in written form, causing the modern-day reader to wonder why only certain issues are addressed while others are apparently left out. It is important to remember that law codes were recorded as guidelines for governing authorities, not for individuals to administer justice privately. The well-known law code of "an eye for an eye" did not grant permission for a man to exact retribution from his neighbor. It provided a guide for a judge handing down a sentence in a case, serving to prevent the wronged party from exacting revenge (overpunishing) instead of receiving what was fair (justice).

Poetry in the Bible, as elsewhere, uses language symbolically and metaphorically to paint word pictures. When a psalmist asks God to utterly destroy his enemies, we can read that as a poetic expression of deep hurt and anger rather than as a really scary prayer request. When an author rhapsodizes that his lover's teeth are like a flock of sheep coming up from the washing, we understand that he means to compliment her on her lovely smile.

Wisdom literature uses language to communicate principles that are generally true, though not universally true. Reading a proverb as a promise can lead to heartache and doubt. Understanding it as a general rule for life can point us toward wise decision-making. The well-known proverb "Train up a child in the way that he should go; even when he is old, he will not depart from it" does not promise that Christian parenting will produce Christian children. Rather, it states the general, wise principle that a godly parent must train her children in the way of godliness.

Prophecy, like poetry, uses language in symbolic ways. Placing a prophecy in its historical and cultural context further clarifies its use of language. When a prophecy says that the sun, moon, and stars will fall from heaven, we can examine this language according to the rules of the genre rather than assuming that a cosmic event is specifically being prophesied (though it may be). Knowing that pagans in ancient cultures worshipped the sun, moon, and stars helps us better understand a prophecy about the demise of the heavenly bodies: the worship of other deities will cease when the prophecy is fulfilled.

5. Why Was It Written?

Every author writes with a specific purpose in mind. The authors of the Bible are no exception; they write to record history, to instruct, to admonish, to inspire, to rebuke, to warn, and to encourage. They write to address the needs, hopes, or fears of their audience in light of the character of God. We can identify why a book was written by considering its major themes and repeated ideas in light of its original audience and its historical and cultural context. Knowing the purpose for which a text was written guards us from reading it solely for our own purposes.

Don't Panic

Here's a piece of good news: no one expects you to know the answers to the five questions off the top of your head, nor should you expect the Holy Spirit to simply reveal the answers to you. He has revealed them, but he has done so by gifting some within the body of believers with the desire and the ability to find those answers through diligent scholarship. You are allowed to get help with archaeology.

But where should you go for help? A reliable study Bible, like the *ESV Study Bible*, will prove an indispensable starting point. A reliable study Bible is an essential tool for someone who wants to start building Bible literacy. At the beginning of each book you will find a discussion of the archaeology questions. Before you begin to read a particular book, read the introductory material found there. But don't just read it—write out the five questions we have posed and note the answers you find to each of them. For the book of Genesis, your notes might look something like this:

Who wrote it?	Authorship is attributed to Moses, Israel's deliverer, law-giver, judge. Probably used existing oral and written sources to write it.
When was it written?	Sometime around 1400 BC, during the forty-year period of wandering in the desert.
To whom was it written?	To the Israelites who were led out of Egypt, during their time in the desert.
In what style was it written?	Generally, historical narrative. Some poetry and prophecy.
Why was it written?	To give the nation of Israel a history and a rule of life as they enter Canaan. To remind them of their past and prepare them for their future.

By writing out the questions and answers yourself, you will better be able to remember what you learned from the introductory material. It's an extra step, but it's worth the effort. A study Bible is not the only place you can find introductory material—a commentary or Bible handbook will also be a help. We will discuss how to choose and use study tools like Bibles and commentaries in the next chapter. For now, bear in mind that it's good to consult more than one source for answers to the five questions. Different scholars answer them in different ways, and not all scholars come from the same theological vantage point. Consulting more than one source helps you to know whether you are answering the five questions the way most scholars who see things from your theological vantage point would answer them.

Ancient and Modern

Just like the city of Rome, your Bible is a modern wonder inseparably linked to an ancient context. Studying with perspective, doing the hard work of digging down to the original cultural and historical framework of a text, enables you to read it the way its human author intended it to be read. Taking into account the original purpose of a book and gaining an appreciation for the literary genre or genres it utilizes enables you to begin the process of building Bible literacy in earnest. Once you have excavated the answers to the five archaeological questions, you are ready to begin the process of learning the text, methodically working to bring ancient treasures into modern contexts.

5

Study with Patience

> As for [the seed] in the good soil, they are those who, hearing the word, hold it fast in an honest and good heart, and bear fruit with patience.
>
> Luke 8:15

So far, we have given thought to the importance of studying with *purpose*—working to place any given text within the Big Story of the Bible, and we have considered the importance of studying with *perspective*—working to place any given text in its original historical and cultural context. These first two *P's* of the Five P's of Sound Study may require greater time and effort to put into practice than we've given to our study in the past, but they will dramatically impact our understanding of what we read. They require more of us as students than we may have thought to give, left to our own devices. Bible study, like most skills of any value, requires discipline. If you have ever had to learn a skill, you will probably remember the frustration that accompanies it—the feelings of inadequacy, the monotony of repeating a process until you have learned it, the strong desire to quit or to find an easier way. Learning to study the Bible well introduces all of these same feelings, which is why our third *P* of sound study is a reminder to let the learning process take its course. In addition to studying with purpose and perspective, we must study with *patience*.

We learn very early from parents and teachers that patience is a virtue. We can see its value in dealing with people or difficulties. We are aware that it shows up as number four in the fruits of the Spirit (Gal. 5:22–23), but we are not always quick to put it into practice. Our culture believes that patience is a hassle and looks for ways to keep us from ever having to exercise it. Television shows resolve conflict in thirty minutes or less. Restaurants serve us food almost as quickly as we can order it. The Internet delivers any and every purchase we could conceive of in under forty-eight hours. Music, e-books, and movies are available instantly. Weight-loss programs offer immediate results. The concept of delaying gratification can be difficult to learn and practice in a patience-optional culture that celebrates immediate satiation of every desire.

So it isn't surprising that the desire for instant gratification can even creep into our study of the Bible. The preponderance of devotional material available to us bears evidence to our love for the neatly-wrapped package: a spiritual insight paired with a few verses and an application point or two. We approach our "time in the Word" like the drive-through at McDonald's: "I've only got a few minutes. Give me something quick and easy to fill me up."

But sound Bible study is rooted in a celebration of delayed gratification. Gaining Bible literacy requires allowing our study to have a cumulative effect—across weeks, months, years—so that the interrelation of one part of Scripture to another reveals itself slowly and gracefully, like a dust cloth slipping inch by inch from the face of a masterpiece. The Bible does not want to be neatly packaged into three-hundred-and-sixty-five-day increments. It does not want to be reduced to truisms and action points. It wants to introduce dissonance into your thinking, to stretch your understanding. It wants to reveal a mosaic of the majesty of God one passage at a time, one day at a time, across a lifetime. By all means, bring eagerness to your study time. Yes, bring hunger. But certainly bring patience—come ready to study for the long term.

Patience with Yourself

Seventh grade was the year the crying began. With the oldest child, we were caught a little off guard—school had never caused this level of upset before. But with the introduction of pre-algebra, all four children adopted a nightly ritual of frustration and tears. Jeff and I developed a mantra, borrowed from a favorite baseball movie: "There is no crying in math."[1] It became the opening salvo in a nightly tutorial in which we would untangle the confusion that had wrapped itself around the day's homework assignment, reassuring the children that they had what it took to complete the work and gently guiding them to patiently press on through the material.

The first time we invoked "There is no crying in math,"

spoken with complete calm to an irrational subject, the subject cried even harder: *You don't understand! I'm completely lost. My teacher did a bad job explaining the concept. The class is too hard. Why didn't you let me enroll in "Outdoor Trails" instead?*

But by the time our youngest entered seventh grade, this scene played out differently. As the baby of the family sat at the table wiping away the first tears of math-induced frustration, I invoked the time-honored mantra: "Calvin. There is no crying in math." And before he could hide it, a smile began to tug at the corners of his mouth. Calvin had the advantage of knowing how seventh grade ended. Having watched his siblings go from tears to smiles during their own seventh grade math adventure, he knew that frustration was a natural part of the learning process. Was there crying in math? Truth to tell, there was plenty of it. But ultimately, Calvin had witnessed diligence and patience do their work as each of his siblings acquired the skills necessary to conquer math—seventh grade and otherwise. Calvin might feel lost now, but the feeling will not last. To feel the frustration of the learning process was to take his place among the siblings who had gone before. Yes, weeping might last for the night, but the joy of understanding would no doubt come with time and effort.

I wish more women understood this perspective when it comes to learning the Bible. Being a student of any subject requires effort—the process of gaining understanding is not easy and can often be frustrating. Depending on the subject, learning may be enjoyable, but it will not be effortless. Learning requires work. This is as true of learning the

Bible as it is of learning algebra. We think that learning the Bible should be as natural as breathing in and out; if knowing God's Word is so good for us, surely he would not make it difficult for us to do so. But learning the Bible requires discipline, and discipline is something we don't naturally embrace. Because learning the Bible is a discipline, patience will play a much-needed role in our progress.

Many classes at my children's schools would never cause them to cry tears of frustration. Classes like Outdoor Trails are fun; they deliver new knowledge to a student, but they may not stretch his understanding. Arriving at understanding is much harder than simply taking in new facts. When we read a newspaper, we do not feel frustrated in our ability to understand it. This is because a newspaper does not intend to stretch our understanding—it is a delivery system for information. Learning the Bible is a quest for knowledge, but it is ultimately a quest for understanding. Unlike a newspaper, the Bible is far more than a delivery system for information—it aims to shape the way we think. This means that, more often than not, we should expect to experience frustration when we sit down to read it.

Do you expect to be met with frustration when you study the Bible? How do you react to the dissonance you feel when your understanding is not equal to a passage? As adults, we no longer must stick to a course of study because a teacher or parent is holding us accountable. If we give in to impatience with the learning process, we tend to react in one of two ways.

We give up. Finding studying the Bible to be too confusing, many of us think "this must not be my area of gifting," and we move on to aspects of our faith that come more naturally. We allow sermons, podcasts, books, or blogs to be our sole source of intake for the Bible. We may read the Bible devotionally, but we assume that we are just not wired to learn it in any sort of structured way.

We look for a shortcut. Wanting to remove as quickly as possible our sense of feeling lost in a text, we run to the notes in our study Bible immediately after reading it. Or we keep a commentary handy so we can consult it at the first signs of confusion. And thanks to the Internet, help is never far away. If we read something confusing, there is no need for tears of frustration—we can simply read what the note in our study Bible says or look up an answer to our question online. But is having interpretive help readily available as helpful as it seems? Or do we end up like those kids in high school English who never actually read a book because the CliffsNotes or the movie was easily available? In reality, using a shortcut is only marginally better than giving up because it does not honor the learning process. By hurrying to eliminate the dissonance of the "I don't know" moment, it actually diminishes the effectiveness of the "aha moment" of discovery.

How Patience Promotes Learning

We love "aha moments"—those moments when something that has confused us suddenly makes sense. What we sometimes overlook about "aha moments" is that they occur after a significant period of feeling lost. Could it be that those periods of feeling lost were actually preparing us for the understanding that was eventually going to come? Could it be that feeling lost is one way God humbles us when we come to his Word, knowing that in due time he will exalt our understanding?

Contrary to our gut reaction, feeling lost or confused is not a bad sign for a student. It is actually a sign that our understanding is being challenged and that learning is about to take place. Embracing the dissonance of feeling lost, rather than avoiding it (giving up) or dulling it (looking for a shortcut), will actually place us in the best possible position to learn. We must extend ourselves permission to get lost and patience to find our way to understanding.

Several years ago I moved from Houston to Dallas. Having lived in Houston for thirteen years, I could drive its streets with ease. I had no idea how to navigate Dallas, so I used a GPS to get everywhere I needed to go. It was a great feeling—knowing almost nothing of the city, I could map a route to my destination instantaneously. I never had to feel lost or waste time wandering around on the wrong roads.

But three years later, I still didn't know my way around Dallas without that GPS. If its battery died or if I left home without it, I was in big trouble. And then another strange thing happened: I took a trip back to Houston. In a city I knew well, I found that my GPS didn't always pick the route that made the most sense. It still spoke with the same tone of authority it used in Dallas, but I could tell that it was choosing a route other than the most direct one.

When I got back to Dallas, I knew what I had to do: I had

to allow myself to get lost. I had to wander around a bit, plan extra travel time, miss some exits, and make wrong turns in order to learn for myself the routes my GPS had spoon-fed me. Guess what? I learned better routes.

This is the same lesson I have learned about the readily available help of commentaries and study Bibles. If I am not careful, they can mask my ignorance of Scripture and give me a false sense that I know my way around its pages. I do not labor for understanding, because the moment I hit a hard passage, I immediately resolve my discomfort of feeling lost by glancing down at the notes or searching a commentary for an answer. And hearing their authoritative tone, I can grow forgetful that they are, in fact, only man's words—an educated opinion, profitable but not infallible.

In short, if I never allow myself to get lost, I never allow the learning process to take its proper course. If I never fight for interpretation on my own, I might accept whatever interpretation I am given at face value. And that's a dangerous route to drive.

My intent is not to question the value of commentary. Sound commentary is invaluable to the Bible student. My intent is to question its place in the learning process. Unless we consult it *after* we attempt to comprehend and interpret on our own, we tend to defer completely to its reasoning. The problem is not with our study Bibles or commentaries; the problem is with our need for instant gratification and our dislike of feeling lost. Commentaries hold a valid place in the learning process, as we will see in our next chapter. But that place is not at the beginning of the learning process, where they can diminish our sense of feeling lost—a feeling that is actually our friend.

The Cumulative Effect of Patient Study

Studying with patience requires taking a long-term view. Allowing yourself to get lost in a text means there will be days when your study time may leave you more confused than you were when you started. For those of us accustomed to having a daily quiet time that inspires us to begin our day, allowing dissonance to linger and to push us to deeper study will be difficult. We might not find a neatly-wrapped application point at the end of every study time, and we may be tempted to think that our time has been profitless without it. But we couldn't be more wrong.

For years I viewed my interaction with the Bible as a debit account: I had a need, so I went to the Bible to withdraw an answer. But we do much better to view our interaction with the Bible as a savings account: I stretch my understanding daily, I deposit what I glean, and I patiently wait for it to accumulate in value, knowing that one day I will need to draw on it. Bible study is an investment with a long-term payoff. Rather than reading a specific text to try to meet an immediate need, give the benefits of your study permission to be stored away for future use. What if the passage you are fighting to understand today suddenly makes sense to you when you most need it, ten years from now? It has been said that we overestimate what we can accomplish in one year and underestimate what we can accomplish in ten. Are you willing to invest ten years in waiting for understanding?

Are you willing to wait a decade for an application point to emerge? Be encouraged that you are storing up treasure, even if you don't see or feel it in the short-term.

This is not to say that there will be no short-term benefits to your study. There will be. My son will not have to complete a degree in higher mathematics to begin to enjoy the benefits of having mastered seventh grade math. But seventh grade math is a long-term investment in his ability to grasp higher levels of understanding. Studying the book of James may immediately show me the benefits of being quick to listen, slow to speak, and slow to become angry. But the ensuing years will no doubt write those lessons deeper and deeper on my heart.

Patience with Circumstances

If I were you, I might be getting a little irritated with me by now. You may be thinking, "I'd love to have patience with the learning process, but exactly when am I supposed to find the time to *begin* a learning process, much less patiently pursue it?" Women cannot always rely on life giving them ample opportunity to study the Bible. A new job, a young family, an aging parent who needs care—any number of circumstances can usher us into a season where time with our Bibles happens in stolen moments at irregular intervals.

For me, these seasons have sometimes lasted for years—sermons and podcasts were a lifeline. Having a structured group study to go to helped keep me in contact with the Bible, but some months even that was too much for me to take on. Some months, just keeping body and soul together for myself and my family seemed to occupy almost every waking moment. I don't consider those months to have been lost time or setbacks to my growth. They were times to employ patience, not with active learning of the Scriptures, but with waiting on the Lord. They deepened my desire for study. Some of my most fruitful times of teaching and writing occurred immediately after just such a period of waiting.

If a life stage is making it difficult for you to set aside regular time for study—either with a group or in your own personal efforts, please hear me say this: That's okay. Give the Lord what you can and trust that he will honor your faithfulness in the small things. Trust that the Lord knows your circumstances better than you do and that he sees your desire to learn and grow. And trust that those times are being used to mature you—to teach you that it is a privilege to be able to devote yourself to learning and studying, and to write more deeply on your heart the truths you have already learned.

Patience and Fruitfulness

The first parable that Jesus ever tells his disciples talks about patience and fruitfulness. If you have spent any time in church, you are most likely familiar with it. Jesus describes a farmer who goes out to sow seed. The seed falls in various places where it cannot grow well, but at last, some falls into fertile soil, where it bears a miraculous harvest. Notice the interpretation that Jesus gives for this climactic moment in the parable: "As for [the seed] in the good soil, they are those who, hearing the word, hold it fast in an honest and good heart, and bear fruit with patience" (Luke 8:15).

When my children were little, they loved the Frog and Toad stories by Arnold Lobel. In one of them, Toad plants seeds to grow a garden. Because he has never gardened before, he watches obsessively for his seeds to sprout as soon as he has planted them, expecting a garden to instantly appear. He plays the violin for them. He sings to them. He reads stories and poems to them. After every attempt to aid the process, he shouts, "Now seeds, start growing!" In due time, according to their own schedule, they do just that.

Unlike Toad in Lobel's tale, the farmer in Jesus's parable shows no anxiety for his seeds. The children of God have hearts of fertile soil. We are able to hear and receive the Word, and when patience has done its work, to bear much fruit. Be patient as you practice the discipline of sound study. Allow the seed of the Word to germinate and grow according to God's good timing, trusting that a miraculous harvest will yield in due time.

6

Study with Process

> Prepare your work outside; get everything ready for yourself in the field, and after that build your house.
>
> Prov. 24:27

We have been learning to build Bible literacy by studying with *purpose*, *perspective*, and *patience*. But as with any building project, a good *process* is also required.

The process I am going to outline here is different from what you might find in a typical "packaged" study. Many studies ask you to read a portion of Scripture and reflect, after which they offer thoughts on its proper interpretation and application. The process I want to introduce asks you, the student, to carry the burden of not just reading, but *owning* the text, and then of attempting interpretation and application on your own. Only after you have done so will this process direct you to look to the opinions and scholarship of others for help.

I'm a fairly creative person. I would rather sketch freehand than trace methodically; I like playing the piano by ear better than by reading music; I like to sew without following a pattern; I like to plant my flowers all willy-nilly instead of evenly spaced; and I like to cook without measuring anything. It may not surprise you that my results can be a little hit-or-miss.

My husband Jeff, on the other hand, is a master of process. He comes from a family of process-driven people who do things the right way for the sheer satisfaction of doing so. There is a right way to do whatever needs to be done, the Wilkin family knows that way, and they will do it exactly that way, no matter how hard it is or how long it takes. There is a proper way to fold towels, to organize a pantry, to trim a hedge, to clean a paintbrush. I have affectionately dubbed this the Wilkin Way. I and my entire crooked-towel-folding family of people-who-would-rather-just-buy-another-paintbrush-than-clean-one-out, find the Wilkin Way both magnificent and incomprehensible.

Let's just say the early years of my marriage provided an opportunity for me to learn and grow.

I like to think Jeff has grown in his appreciation for the happy accidents and unexpected genius I have contributed to meals, Halloween costumes, and the occasional gardening triumph. I have certainly grown in my appreciation for honoring a process. I have watched the Wilkin Way result in beautifully refinished furniture, meticulously painted rooms, perfectly crafted decks, immaculately manicured lawns, and barbecue that will make you weep just to taste it.

The world needs both willy-nilly creatives and process-driven builders. Both contribute their strengths to the body of believers. But Bible literacy is closer to a building project than an art project. If you were building a house, you would hire a builder who observes process, not one who thinks building codes are "great suggestions." You would want a builder who subscribes to the Wilkin Way of thinking. And that's the kind of builder you and I must become in order to build Bible literacy. We must be those who build on the rock-solid foundation of mind-engaging process, rather than on the shifting sands of "what this verse means to me" subjectivity.

How should we build our understanding of Scripture? By what orderly process? A good literacy-builder honors the learning process by moving through three distinct stages of understanding: *comprehension*, *interpretation*, and *application*. Each of the three stages seeks to answer a specific question about the text.

1. *Comprehension* asks, "What does it say?"
2. *Interpretation* asks, "What does it mean?"
3. *Application* asks, "How should it change me?"

We actually move through these stages intuitively in our everyday lives; we use them all the time to process information. Anyone who wakes up to an alarm in the morning has moved from comprehension to interpretation to application:

- In a deep sleep, we become aware of a sound. At first, our brain may ignore the sound or incorporate it into whatever dream we are having. As the sound repeats, our brain recognizes "my alarm is going off." We have *comprehended* the sound. It is not the smoke detector, it is not part of a dream—it is our alarm.

- Once we realize we are hearing our alarm, our brain *interprets* its meaning: "It is 7 a.m."
- We then *apply* what our sleepy brain has comprehended and interpreted: "It is time for me to get up and start my day."

In this simple, everyday example, we move from comprehension to interpretation to application so quickly that we are probably not aware the first two stages have even taken place. With Bible study, each stage requires more deliberate effort and considerably more time. Notice, too, that each stage will operate within the framework of the purpose, perspective, and patience we have already set in place.

- We will need to reflect on the purpose of our study, allowing the three stages to help us place our text within the Big Story.
- We will need to employ the perspective of our five archaeological questions to help us with comprehension and interpretation.
- We will need to draw on the patience we discussed in the previous chapter to help us resist the urge to rush straight to application.

Now let's consider how each of the three stages functions within the context of Bible study as an orderly process for building literacy.

Stage 1: Comprehension—"What Does It Say?"

The comprehension stage is probably the most neglected and misunderstood by students of the Bible, mainly because we assume that reading a text and absorbing a sense of its message equates to comprehending it. Because of this misconception, we will take our time discussing what comprehension is and how it is reached. If you have read other books about Bible study, you may have heard the first step in the learning process termed as "observation" rather than "comprehension." I believe *comprehension* better captures what we want to accomplish. Observation can be subjective—it can connote a casual perusal, in which I pull out details or thoughts that seem significant to me as I read. Comprehension, on the other hand, is more objective. It seeks purposefully to discover what the original author *intended* me to notice or ask.

Remember the reading comprehension section on the SAT? Remember those long reading passages followed by questions to test your knowledge of what you had just read? The objective of those questions was to force you to read for detail. This is exactly how we should begin our study of a text. Asking ourselves "What does it say?" is hard work, and it requires us to slow down when we read. A person who comprehends the account of the six days of creation in Genesis 1 can tell you specifically what happened on each day. This first step of comprehending what the text says moves us toward being able to interpret and apply the story of creation to our lives.

A good builder uses good tools. What are the tools we can use to begin to build comprehension of a passage? I want to suggest six:

1. A Printed Copy of the Text

If you were to look through the books on my bookshelves, it would not take you long to figure out which ones are the most loved. A worn spine might be your first hint, but flipping through the pages would quickly reveal my favorites: the margins are covered in handwriting, favorite paragraphs are highlighted, beautiful phrases are underlined, ideas I disagree with are marked with a giant cross-hatch and an answering thought. But if you opened my Bible, you would see pristine pages—no handwritten notes at all. Why don't I take notes in the most important book I own? Because there isn't enough room.

You will never mark those gold-edged, small-print, tissue-thin pages in your Bible the way they deserve to be marked. When you begin study of a text, print out a double-spaced copy in a 12-point font on nice, thick printer paper. Print a copy that will give you the space and the freedom to mark repeated words, phrases, or ideas, and even to write "What does this MEAN?????" in giant red letters in the margin. Print a copy that will allow you to annotate the text as a true student would. Go ahead and treat yourself to a nice set of colored pencils and a new highlighter while you're at it. More on that in a bit.

Using a printed copy of the text for comprehension will also help you to resist the urge to glance at the notes in your study Bible. Feel free to print your copy with the cross-references included. We'll be using them.

2. Repetitive Reading

Now that you have your markable copy of the text, you are ready to begin reading repetitively. The historical, cultural, and linguistic gap that exists between the Bible and its modern-day reader makes repetitive reading a critical tool in our attempts to build comprehension. Simply put, we are probably not going to catch what the author intended to communicate in one reading. The first step in comprehending a text is reading it several times from start to finish. We wouldn't expect to read once through a scene in Shakespeare's *King Lear* and come away with a clear understanding of what it says. Nor should we expect to be able to do so with the Bible. Having armed ourselves with historical and cultural context (by reading the introductory material in a study Bible and answering the five archaeological questions), we begin reading, attempting to hear the text with the ears of its original hearers.

How many times should we read a text? As many as we need to. For a shorter book of the Bible, I ask the women in my studies to read through the entire book each week before they begin to look at the specific passage we are covering. This means they may have read the book of James at least eleven times by the end of the study. For longer books, reading the entire book two or three times before incorporating the other comprehension tools is usually sufficient. Be honest about your own skill level. If you are new to reading the Bible for comprehension, you may need more initial read-throughs than someone who has used the tool longer.

Repetitive reading offers two main benefits to the student: Scripture memory and overall familiarity with a text. For those of us who don't love memorizing Scripture, repetitive reading is an excellent way to internalize the words. I call it the "lazy method" of Scripture memorization. But of course, it isn't really lazy at all—it's intuitive. Repetition is the very first learning strategy we employ as children; it is how we learn to speak, to recite the Pledge of Allegiance, and to quote our favorite movie lines. Repetitive reading helps us to memorize Scripture in the best way possible—within its original context. We may not memorize an entire passage, but the verses that begin to lodge in our memory will do so as part of our larger understanding of the entire book we are reading. Any time we memorize a verse without knowing what comes before or after it, we run the very real danger of misapplying it.

Ultimately, we gain general familiarity with the text with repetitive reading. The more we read through a book or lengthy passage, the more it will reveal its general structure and themes to us, enabling us to employ the next comprehension tool in our toolbox: outlining. Keep in mind that we read repetitively at the outset of a study to get a *general* sense of the text—this is the starting point for comprehension. Repetitive reading does not require that we agonize over meaning or look for ways to apply truth. It simply serves as an introduction, like the first three or four conversations we have with a new acquaintance.

3. Annotation

After your first read-through, begin marking your copy of the text on subsequent readings to get a better feel for what it says.

- Are certain words, phrases, or ideas repeated? Use your colored pencils to mark them distinctly on your printed copy. You can develop any notation system you like—circling, boxing, different kinds of underlines, icons. Just be consistent and do what works intuitively for you.

- Is a particular attribute of God illustrated or celebrated? Write it in the margin.
- Does the text make several points in a row? Number each point as it is introduced in the text.
- Are there words you don't understand? Mark them with a question mark so you can look up a definition for them.
- Are there key transition words, such as *if/then*, *therefore*, *likewise*, *but*, *because*, or *in the same way*? Draw an arrow to connect a concluding thought to its beginning argument.
- Is an idea confusing? Write your question in the margin to address at a later time.

4. An English Dictionary

Use an English dictionary to look up unfamiliar words, or even familiar words that bear a closer examination. Yes, that's right—a plain old English dictionary. Could you use a Hebrew-Greek lexicon? You could, if you know what you're doing. Many of us don't, but the English dictionary can be a great help. Translators choose English words with great care. Our comprehension of what the text is saying can be enhanced simply by looking up a difficult word in the English dictionary. One of the most common ways we rush through the comprehension stage is by assuming that we understand the definitions of the words we are reading. We might take the time to look up *propitiation*, but do we take the time to look up more familiar words such as *holy*, *sanctify*, *honor*, or *perseverance*? By slowing down and considering the meanings of key words or unfamiliar words, we move toward comprehension. Look up the word in question and then, based on the context, come up with a definition that best fits the way it is used in the text. Then note that definition in the margin of your printed copy.

5. Other Translations of the Bible

Reading a passage in more than one translation can expand your understanding of its meaning. If you typically use the ESV, comparing a difficult verse to another translation such as the NIV, NASB, NKJV, or RSV can sometimes help clear up confusion. It is important to note that there is a difference between a translation and a paraphrase. Translations stick closely to the original language. They preserve the "what does it say?" of the Hebrew and Greek as they translate these languages word-for word or thought-for thought into English. Paraphrases, such as the NLT or *The Message*, attempt to take the original language and ask, "What does it mean?" They interpret. Paraphrases can be useful but should be regarded as commentary (man's interpretation of God's words). Paraphrases are best consulted after careful study of an actual translation. Because of this, we will save them for our next step in the process.

6. Outlining

Once you have read through a text a few times, annotated it, looked up word definitions, and compared translations, you can begin to organize what you are reading into an outline. When we attempt to outline, we acknowledge that the original author wrote with a purpose in mind, and we try to identify that purpose.

You don't have to be a Bible scholar to write an outline. Give it your best shot, and then compare what you came up with to what scholars have to say. Look for main points and the subpoints that support them. Not all books of the Bible can be neatly outlined—sometimes the chronology of a story is confusing, or sometimes an author addresses a topic in more than one passage. Your outline does not need to be exhaustive. Its purpose is to help you recognize the overall structure and purpose of the text, not capture every single idea. You can also revise your outline as your study progresses and your familiarity with the text grows. At the conclusion of my study, I often look back at my initial outline and see better ways to organize the text.

Repetitive reading, annotating a printed copy of the text, defining key words, comparing translations, and outlining can all help us with the critical first step of understanding "what does it say?" Just comprehending what the text says is a worthwhile goal for the time you spend in study. Proper comprehension is what enables proper interpretation and application to occur.

Stage 2: Interpretation—"What Does It Mean?"

While comprehension asks, "What does it say?" interpretation asks, "What does it mean?" Now that we have made the effort to understand the structure, language, and details of the text, we are ready to look into its meaning. A person who *comprehends* the account of the six days of creation in

Genesis 1 can tell you specifically what happened on each day. A person who *interprets* the creation story can tell you why God created in a particular order or way. She is able to deduce things from the text beyond what it says.

Most of us rely on sermons, study Bible notes, and commentaries to help us with interpretation. This is appropriate. We have already discussed their necessity for helping us answer the five archaeological questions. God gifts certain people among us with unique knowledge and understanding, and we would be fools to overlook their contributions to our study. They provide an indispensible service to the body of believers. But we must always keep in view that each of us individually is called to love God with our minds. This means that it is good for us to earnestly attempt interpretation on our own before we read the interpretations of others. And this means we must wait to consult commentaries, study Bibles, podcasts, blogs, and paraphrases for interpretative help until we have taken our best shot at interpreting on our own.

So, before we help ourselves to these study aids, two tools in particular will help us craft our own interpretation.

1. Cross-References

Cross-references are the verses listed in the margins or at the bottom of the page in your Bible. They identify commonalities between different parts of the Bible—similar themes, words, events, or people. You may have heard the expression "let Scripture interpret Scripture." This is the most basic principle of interpretation; it's the idea that the best way to grasp what a Bible text is saying is by looking at other places in the Bible that say the same or similar things. Cross-references help us to honor this basic principle and should serve as the starting point for answering, "What does it mean?" When you encounter a passage that is hard to understand, look up the cross-references first to see what they can add to your understanding.

2. Paraphrasing

Paraphrasing is the skill of writing someone else's thoughts in your own words. Of all the tools mentioned thus far, I believe paraphrasing is the hardest. It requires us to slow down and employ patience. If we find paraphrasing to be easy, we are probably not giving it the focus it deserves. If we invest in it, we grow in our maturity as a student.

When you encounter a verse or passage that is hard to understand, check the context, check any tricky words in the dictionary, check the cross-references, and then write out the passage in your own words. Paraphrasing helps you focus on what is being said. Even if your paraphrase is not great, it will force you to read for detail and meaning. You don't have to share it with anyone—it is a tool for your own use. Once you do consult a commentary, you may decide your paraphrase is awful. That's okay. By forcing you to wrestle through the text, the exercise will have accomplished what it needs to.

Once we have earnestly attempted comprehension and interpretation on our own, we are ready to consider the interpretations of others. Attempting to interpret on our own before consulting commentary is vital because no two commentaries say the same thing. Doing the personal work of comprehension and interpretation helps us discern which commentaries are reliable, which interpretation best fits with what the text says. It takes time to be able to recognize which authors and teachers you can trust for thoughtful, reliable interpretation. Ask a seasoned teacher or your pastor for recommendations to start building a personal library of trusted commentators. When you find a commentator you love, search his or her footnotes for more potential good sources.

Stage 3: Application—"How Should It Change Me?"

At last, we arrive at the step in the learning process where our hard work translates into action. After establishing what the text says and what the text means, we are finally in a position to ask how it should impact us. Application asks, "How should the text change me?"

In chapter 1 we acknowledged that the Bible is a book about God. When we apply a text, we must remind ourselves once more that the knowledge of God and the knowledge of self always go hand in hand, that there is no true knowledge of self apart from the knowledge of God. Understood from a God-centered perspective, the question, "How should the text change me?" is answered by asking three subquestions:

- What does this passage teach me about God?
- How does this aspect of God's character change my view of self?
- What should I do in response?

A person who *comprehends* the account of the six days of creation in Genesis 1 can tell you specifically what happened on each day. A person who *interprets* the creation story can tell you why God created in a particular order or way. A person who *applies* the creation story can tell you that because God creates in an orderly fashion, we too should live well-ordered lives (more on this later). Knowledge of God gleaned through comprehension of the text and interpretation of its meaning can now be applied to life in a way that challenges the student to be different.

Why Studying with Process Is Worth the Effort

Studying with process allows us to uncover the character of God in Scripture through careful comprehension and interpretation. It then allows us to properly apply Scripture in light of who God has revealed himself to be. Does the comprehension-interpretation-application process sound hard? It may be at first, but it becomes more intuitive the more you use it. It is the process for an orderly, long-term building project with cumulative benefits. Even if you are in a season of life that won't allow you to use all the tools of the process exhaustively, you can use them as far as your time does allow. Build slowly if you must, but by all means, build. In pursuing an orderly process, you follow a pattern established by God himself.

The God of the Bible is a God of order. In fact, the first and final scenes recorded for us in Scripture show God ordering the cosmos. Genesis 1–3 shows God ordering a garden, taking that which was formless and empty and giving it both form and function in six orderly steps, rendering it a perfectly ordered dwelling for his presence. Revelation 21 shows God reordering the disorder of a fallen world in the form of a new heaven and a new earth, culminating in the unveiling of the New Jerusalem, a perfectly ordered dwelling for his presence.

If you are familiar with the book of Exodus, you know that it, too, contains a story of orderly creation. God commands Israel to create a perfectly ordered tabernacle through an orderly process, that he might take up residence within its curtained walls. Page after page is devoted to detailing the process for building the structure, the end result of which is a beautiful place in which God and man can commune. Unlike the creation stories of Eden and the New Jerusalem in which God alone creates, God involves humans in the orderly work of creating the tabernacle. He invites them into the process. The stories of the building of Solomon's temple in 1 Kings and the rebuilding of Jerusalem in Ezra and Nehemiah speak of other times when humans become participants in the creative, orderly process of establishing or reestablishing a place of fellowship with God. And as temples of the Holy Spirit (1 Cor. 6:19–20), *you and I are called to become participants in the process* of creating and maintaining an orderly, beautiful place within our hearts where the Lord may dwell. One of the most important ways we do this is through Bible study.

The sovereign God of the universe once dwelt with us in a perfectly ordered garden of his own creation. He will one day dwell with us again in a perfectly ordered city of his own creation. But in the space between these two bookends, we are granted unique opportunities to be involved in the orderly work of creating spaces where the divine and the human can share fellowship together. Studying the Bible with process is a means to do just that.

We may begin the work of building as rather sloppy builders, but we have a faithful God who is patient with his workers and who equips them with all they need to do the work at hand. We have only to ask for what we need. With that in mind, we are ready to consider the final *P* of sound Bible study: study with prayer.

7

Study with Prayer

> If any of you lacks wisdom, let him ask God, who gives generously to all without reproach, and it will be given him.
>
> James 1:5

We often hear that good things come in small packages. I am praying that this will be true of the small chapter you are about to read. Don't let the word count fool you: Though more space has been devoted to the four *P's* that have come before, this fifth and final *P* of sound study is no less important. In fact, we could argue that *prayer* is the most important of them all. Prayer is the means by which we implore the Holy Spirit to take up residence in our study time. Without prayer, our study is nothing but an intellectual pursuit. With prayer, it is a means of communing with the Lord. Prayer is what changes our study from the pursuit of knowledge to the pursuit of God himself.

You may be familiar with the acronym PART as a memory prompt for the key elements of prayer:

Praise: glorify God for who he is and what he has done.
Admit: confess to God where you have fallen short.
Request: ask God to forgive your sin and to meet your needs.
Thank: give thanks to God for who he is and what he has done.

Let's consider how to incorporate prayer into our study efforts—before, during, and after we study—using PART as our guide. You probably already have a practice of everyday prayer that involves the elements of PART. Your study time offers a unique additional opportunity to tailor your prayers specifically to correspond to the ministry of the Word.

Your prayer time may be long or short. It may be intermittent as you study. Recognize the benefit of praying at all stages of your study, but give yourself room to incorporate it as you are led to do so. Pray from a sincere desire, not from a sense of obligation to "do things the right way." If you lack the desire to pray, confess that to the Lord and ask him to increase that desire within you as you study.

Pray before You Study

Praise: Begin by praising God for giving us the revelation of his will and character in his Word. If you are in the midst of a book, praise him for specific attributes that your study has already revealed. If you are at the beginning of a book, praise him for being merciful and gracious to grant you the gift of the Bible.

Admit: Know your own set of insecurities and weaknesses as you set out to study, and lay them before the Lord. Confess that you can't do it and that it feels too hard. Confess any sin that might inhibit your study (pride? impatience? distraction?). Confess your lack of desire.

Request: Ask the Lord for ears to hear and eyes to see as you study. Ask him to help you guard the time you have set aside from distractions; ask him to clear your mind of other concerns. Ask him to reveal his character and your sin. Ask him to make his Word come alive for you in such a way that you know him better and see your own need of him more clearly.

Thank: Thank him that he has revealed himself in the Bible and that he has given you the ability to know him. Thank him for time to study. Thank him for the gift of Jesus Christ.

Pray during Your Study

Praise: As you study, praise God when you make a connection about his character that you hadn't understood before. Praise him when you notice that you are beginning to ask the right questions of the text on your own. Give him praise when you find yourself enjoying your study, knowing that he is the origin of that joy.

Admit: Confess when you get frustrated with your study. Confess if you find it boring. Tell him what you would rather be doing or what feels more urgent. Confess if you chafe against what the passage is asking of you or showing you.

Request: When you hit a hard passage, ask the Lord to grant understanding. If your mind is wandering, ask for help to stay focused. If you get frustrated, ask him to teach you patience and humility. If you find yourself rushing, ask him to help you slow down. If you are besieged with interruptions, ask him to grant you some peaceful time, or to help you know if it's time to pack it in for the day.

Thank: Thank the Lord when he brings to mind other passages in Scripture that confirm or reinforce what you are learning in your study. Thank him when you receive correction from the text, or when you are given an example to follow. Thank him each time the gospel reveals itself to you through your study.

Pray after You Study

Praise: Meditate on the aspect of God's character that your study is revealing to you. Did the passage show God as merciful? Patient? Generous? Wrathful? Holy? Praise God for this aspect of who he is. If appropriate, pray aloud the passage of Scripture that celebrates that aspect of God's character.

Admit: Confess any personal sin that your study time has brought to light. Confess your temptation to apply the passage to someone else's sin problem instead of your own. Confess if you let yourself get distracted as you studied. Did your study time heighten your awareness of your lack of understanding? Did you rush to finish? Confess that, too.

Request: Ask the Lord to help you apply what you have learned. Did learning that God is gracious reveal your own lack of grace toward someone? Ask the Lord to help you act on what you have learned. Ask him to bring to mind what you have studied as you move through your day and your week. If your study time felt fruitless, ask him to help you trust that there is fruit you cannot yet see. Ask him to give you the desire to persevere in the learning process.

Thank: Thank the Lord for what he is teaching you. Thank him for the gift of personal insight, and for the men and women who have written the commentaries you use. Thank him specifically for a truth he has shown you during your study.

Seem Like a Lot of Praying?

The suggestions for prayer that I have given are just that: suggestions. They do not represent a magical formula of any kind; nor are they an exhaustive list; nor must they fill a certain amount of time. My point is to challenge you to let prayerfulness imbue your study from start to finish. Learning the Bible does not happen as a result of human effort alone. Like all other aspects of our sanctification, it is the result of the Holy Spirit working in and through our efforts.

How much time you spend and how much depth you reach in study-related prayer will depend in some measure on your schedule. There will certainly be days when you whisper, "Help me, Lord!" and charge ahead. But let there also be days when you fully savor the element of prayer throughout your study. The Holy Spirit has a way of speaking through the Scripture whether we ask him to or not. How much better to invite him? To welcome him? To celebrate his presence in our daily study? If the Word of God is truly living and active, it is so because of the ministrations of the Holy Spirit, through the finished work of Christ, by the loving decree of the Father. Prayer invokes the fellowship of the Trinity in your study time, a sweet and necessary fellowship for any student of the Word.

And unlike the length of this chapter, that is no small thing.

8

Pulling It All Together

> With my whole heart I seek you; let me not wander from your commandments! I have stored up your word in my heart, that I might not sin against you.
>
> Ps. 119:10–11

So there you have it: the Five P's of Sound Study, five tools to help you build Bible literacy and thereby grow in your love for the God the Bible proclaims. Here is a quick review of each *P* that sums up what we have learned.

Study with *Purpose*	Understand where your text fits into the Big Story of creation-fall-redemption-restoration
Study with *Perspective*	Understand the "archaeology" of your text (its historical and cultural context)

Study with *Patience*	Resolve not to hurry; set a realistic expectation for your pace of study, focusing on the long term
Study with *Process*	Begin methodically reading for comprehension, interpretation, and application
Study with *Prayer*	Ask the Father to help you before, during, and after your study time

Now that we have the whole study method in view, let's look at how you might actually use it by walking through an example. As I mentioned when I introduced them, the Five P's relation to one another is not strictly linear. They are not a checklist, but a set of practices that interrelate and overlap. No single example will capture exactly how your study might progress, but this chapter should get you started in the right direction. For the purpose of our example, we will assume that *patience* and *prayer* will be required throughout our study. We'll focus our attention on how to study with *purpose*, *perspective*, and *process* using the book of James.

You will notice as you move through this example that each step is not broken down into a specific increment of time. If you are used to having a study guide or a teacher break down the study process into daily or weekly increments for you, not having this structure may take some getting used to. It will also give you freedom to work at your own pace. You can do as much or as little in a given sitting as your time allows. You might take three days or three weeks to read the text through several times, depending on how much time you have. More important than accomplishing a set amount of study is making a steady progress in the right direction, using an approach that will build literacy.

Bearing that in mind, let's walk through how your study might progress if you decided to learn the book of James according to our study method. Before you begin, gather the following items:

- A printed copy of the text, double-spaced and with wide margins. Include the footnotes and cross-references.
- A pen and a highlighter.
- A set of colored pens or pencils for annotating.
- A journal or binder for keeping your notes all in one place.

Step 1: Begin with Purpose

Start your study by considering where the book of James fit into the Big Story of the Bible. What part does it play in telling the story of creation-fall-redemption-restoration? How does it point to the reign and rule of God? Unless you are studying Genesis or Revelation, it can be difficult at the outset of your study to know exactly where the book you have chosen fits into the Big Story. That's okay. Get a general idea as you begin (consult the introductory material in your study Bible or a commentary) and commit to keeping the question in the back of your mind as you go.

As you spend time in the text, its specific contributions to the Big Story will begin to emerge more clearly. By the end of your study, you should be able to point to the themes of the metanarrative as they appear in your text. Because the book of James is New Testament Wisdom Literature (as we'll discover below), it clearly deals with the theme of redemption, specifically progressive sanctification, though other elements of the metanarrative are present as well.

Step 2: Get Perspective on the Book You Will Be Studying

Using a study Bible, trusted commentary, or both, answer the archaeological questions for the book of James. Take your time with this so that once you begin reading, you will be able to listen for how the letter would have been heard by its original audience. In your journal, write out each of the archaeological questions, and note a brief answer for each. You will be able to use your answers as a reference point when you're in step 3. Your answers to the archaeological questions for James might look something like this:

1. Who wrote it?	James, the brother of Jesus. Rose to position of prominence in church at Jerusalem (Acts 15). Known as "James the Just"; known for the amount of time he spent in prayer. Died in AD 62—martyred. Thrown from the temple wall, stoned, and beaten to death.
2. When was it written?	Around AD 49, making it the earliest writing of the New Testament.

3. To whom was it written?	To Jewish Christians enduring persecution, in the earliest days of the church, by one familiar with Old Testament writing and imagery.
4. In what style was it written?	Written like the Wisdom Literature of the O.T.—Proverbs, Job, Song of Solomon. Many exhortations—54 direct calls to obedience. Tone is that of authority, commanding respect.
5. Why was it written?	To show how to live the life of godliness in practical, everyday ways. Answers the question, "What does genuine faith look like?"

If you are unfamiliar with the genre of Wisdom Literature, you might do some additional reading to discover more about it. If some aspect of the historical setting interests you, you might explore it further as well. The more time you spend "getting into the skin" of the original hearers, the more likely you are to navigate comprehension-interpretation-application well.

Step 3: Begin the Process of Comprehension-Interpretation-Application

Comprehension: What Does It Say?

Using your double-spaced copy of the text, read through James from start to finish, paying attention to the footnotes and making notes in the margins summarizing big ideas. Remember to keep in mind James's original hearers as you summarize. What main thoughts would they take from his letter, based on their current circumstance of being persecuted for their faith?

Read through the letter a few more times, annotating repeated words, phrases, or ideas as they begin to emerge in your understanding. Read the letter in two other translations as part of your repetitive reading. As you grow more familiar with what the text says, begin transferring your summary statements into your journal to form a rough outline of the letter. Your general outline of the book of James might look something like this:

- Greetings (1:1).
- Trials and Temptations (1:2–18).
    - It is good for our faith to be tested (1:2–12).
    - We are not tempted by God, but by our desires (1:13–18).
- Don't just listen to the Word, act on what you hear (1:19–27).
- Don't play favorites (2:1–13).
- True faith always results in works (2:14–26).
- Watch your words (3:1–12).
- Two kinds of wisdom (3:13–18).
- Don't give in to worldliness (ch. 4).
    - Don't be quarrelsome (4:1–3).
    - Don't be friends with the world (4:4).
    - Don't be prideful (4:5–10).
    - Don't speak against each other (4:11–12).
    - Don't boast (4:13–17).
- Warning to the unjust rich (5:1–6).
- Closing exhortations (5:7–20).
    - Be patient in suffering (5:7–11).

- Say what you mean (5:12).
- Pray in faith (5:13–18).
- Restore those who wander from the truth (5:19–20).

Don't agonize over the outline. You can always go back and revise it as your study progresses. Once you have a feel for what James is saying in general, begin to look for what he is saying in particular. Begin working through the logical sections of the letter piece by piece.

Your rough outline identified James 1:1–18 as comprising the first two logical sections in the book: the greeting and a discussion of trials and temptations. Look over that portion of the text and mark the following things:

- Does the text contain repeated words, phrases, or ideas?
- Does it mention attributes of God (things that are true about him)?
- Does the text make several points in a row? Number each point as it is introduced in the text.
- Did you come across words you don't understand? Mark them with a question mark. Look them up in the dictionary and write a definition or synonym for them on your copy.
- Does the passage include key transition words, such as *if/then*, *therefore*, *likewise*, *but*, *because*, or *in the same way*? Draw an arrow to connect a concluding thought to its beginning argument.
- Is an idea confusing? Write your question in the margin to address at a later time.

Bearing in mind that each student's annotation will look different, here is what your copy of James 1:1–18 might look like once you have marked it (see sample annotation, pp. 118–19).

Interpretation: What Does It Mean?

Now that you have read closely for comprehension, use cross-references, paraphrasing, and commentary (in that order) to help you arrive at an interpretation.

Cross-References

Look up the cross-references listed in your Bible for each verse in the section you are studying (they will be located in the margin or at the bottom of the page in your Bible). Then note how the cross-referenced passage enhances your understanding of the passage you are studying. For instance, the cross-references listed for James 1:2–3 in the ESV Bible are Matthew 5:12 and 1 Peter 1:6. Look up each cross-reference, and read the surrounding verses so that you can place them in their context. Note who is speaking, and to whom. In this case, we need to read Matthew 5:11–12 (Jesus, the brother of James, addressing the disciples) and 1 Peter 1:6–7 (Peter addressing persecuted Christians) to fully understand the connection of each cross-reference.

> **James 1:2–3:** Count it all joy, my brothers, when you meet trials of various kinds, for you know that the testing of your faith produces steadfastness.

> **Matthew 5:11–12:** Blessed are you when others revile you and persecute you and utter all kinds of evil against you falsely on my account. Rejoice and be glad, for your

reward is great in heaven, for so they persecuted the prophets who were before you.

1 Peter 1:6–7: In this you rejoice, though now for a little while, if necessary, you have been grieved by various trials, so that the tested genuineness of your faith—more precious than gold that perishes though it is tested by fire—may be found to result in praise and glory and honor at the revelation of Jesus Christ.

Notice how the words of Jesus and Peter expand our understanding of the words of James. Trials are ultimately a blessing: they render us a heavenly reward, are relatively brief, prove that our faith is genuine, and bring glory to God.

Paraphrasing

Remember that paraphrasing is just writing a verse or passage in our own words to help us wrestle with its meaning. Paraphrasing is particularly helpful when a verse seems unclear or confusing.

The exhortation in James 1:2–3 to "count it all joy" may seem at first to be telling us that trials should be a source of joy to us as we are enduring them. Is James telling those enduring hard persecution that they should smile and be thrilled about it? When we consult other translations, we find that the NIV reads "consider it pure joy" and the NASB reads "consider it all joy." The thesaurus helps further by showing that *regard* and *reckon* can be synonyms of *count* and *consider*. Our cross-references speak to the idea of persecution resulting in a future reward. Combining these reference points, you might paraphrase James 1:2–3 like

James 1:1-18 ESV

Greeting

slave or bondservant

God has authority

[1]James, a servant of God and of the Lord Jesus Christ,

To the twelve tribes in the Dispersion: ? → Jews scattered throughout Asia Minor

Greetings.

James encourages his readers that trials produce maturity.

Testing of Your Faith

Jesus said this in Matt. 5:12

[2]Count it all joy, my Brothers, when you meet trials of various kinds, [3]for you know that the testing of your faith produces steadfastness. [4]And let steadfastness have its full effect, that you may be perfect and complete, lacking in nothing.

NIV: perseverance

Q: Do I rejoice in trials as I should?

NIV: mature + complete

then

[5]If any of you lacks wisdom, let him ask God, who gives generously to all without reproach, and it will be given him. [6]But let him ask in faith, with no doubting, for the one who doubts is like a wave of the sea that is driven and tossed by the wind. [7]For that person must not suppose that he will receive anything from the Lord; [8] he is a double-minded man, unstable in all his ways.

V5- God is wise and generous

Trials reveal our need for wisdom. God gives wisdom to the one who asks in faith.

God invites us to ask

Q: Am I double-minded? (Jam. 3:13-18) In what areas?

Whether rich or poor, we are all fragile and fleeting.

[9]Let the lowly Brother boast in his exaltation, [10]and the rich in his humiliation, because like a flower of the grass he will pass away. [11]For the sun rises with its scorching heat and withers the grass; its flower falls, and its beauty perishes. So also will the rich man fade away in the midst of his pursuits.

HUH?

V11- Unlike us, God is eternal (see Isa. 40:6-8)

[12]Blessed is the man who remains steadfast
Not "happy," but having the approval and assistance of God himself!
under trial, for when he has stood the test he
will receive the crown of life, which God has
promised to those who love him. [13]Let no one
say when he is tempted, "I am being tempted by
Gen. 3:11-12 — Adam says this
God," for God cannot be tempted with evil, and
he himself tempts no one. [14]But each person is
tempted when he is lured and enticed by his own
desire. [15]Then desire when it has conceived gives
birth to sin, and sin when it is fully grown brings
forth death.

God does not tempt. We allow ourselves to be lured and enticed into sin.

V13- God is never the source of temptation

God makes good on his promises

VV14-15: wrong desires → temptations that appeal to them → sin → death
VV2-4: faith → trials that test it → steadfastness → maturity

[16]Do not be deceived, my beloved Brothers.
[17]Every good gift and every perfect gift is from
above, coming down from the Father of lights
with whom there is no variation or shadow due
to change. [18]Of his own will he brought us forth
Lev. 2:14-16 - what connection?
by the word of truth, that we should be a kind of
Christ!
firstfruits of his creatures.

The world will lie to us about what is good and bad. The One who saved us gives us all that is good.

V16- God tells us the truth.

V17- God gives good and perfect gifts

V17- God is light

V17- God does not change

V18- God brought us forth of his own will

Q: What do I wrongly believe to be a good gift that is not?

Q: What trial have I seen as a bad thing that might ultimately give me the gift of maturity?

this: *My brothers, when you are persecuted, regard it as a source of future joy, knowing that when your faith is tested, you grow in your ability to persevere.*

Is your paraphrase accurate? You'll know better when you begin reading commentary to see if scholars have arrived at a similar conclusion. Either way, you have done your part to attempt interpretation on your own. If you find that your paraphrase was not accurate, just go back and note your improved understanding in your journal or on your copy of the text as your thinking develops.

Consulting Commentary

Having invested the effort to understand what the text says and means on your own, you are now ready to consider what others have to say. You might find it helpful to move from the general to the specific with commentaries. Start with your study Bible notes, and then read more in-depth commentaries or teachings to refine your thinking. Remember to use commentaries from trusted sources. Look for agreement and disagreement among your commentaries. Where they disagree, ask yourself which interpretation fits best with what you yourself have gleaned from your study efforts.

Application: How Should It Change Me?

Once you have done the work of comprehension and interpretation, you're ready to consider how to apply what you have been learning. Recall that the question "how should the text change me?" is answered by asking three subquestions:

- What does this passage teach me about God?

- How does this aspect of God's character change my view of self?
- What should I do in response?

Looking back at your notes in the margin for James 1:1–18, you are now ready to take what you have observed about God's character and draw application from it. Our example shows several truths about God noted in the margin. Transfer these notes to your journal, writing out a corresponding view of self and a response for each one:

1. *View of God:* God (Jesus) has authority (1:1).
   View of Self: I do not hold authority over my life or my circumstances.
   Response: How can I better submit to Jesus as Lord? In what area of my life am I attempting to hold onto control?

2. *View of God:* God has wisdom. He gives it generously when we ask (1:5).
   View of Self: I lack wisdom. I operate out of my own wisdom rather than asking him for godly wisdom.
   Response: In what areas of my life do I most need godly wisdom right now? Have I asked for it?

We can and should draw other application points from the text, but we must remember that the God-centered questions should *always* be our starting point. They should never be an afterthought. Examples of other application points that might arise from your initial consideration of the character of God in James 1:1–18 include:

- James, who called Jesus "brother" during his life, opens his letter by calling Jesus "Lord" and "Christ." Do I show respect to Jesus as Lord Christ, or do I think of him too casually?
- God gives wisdom (1:5) and every good and perfect gift (1:16). Have I asked for wisdom? Have I thanked God for the good gifts he has given me?

Your application questions can form the basis of a closing prayer. Or, if you are gathering with other women to discuss, these questions can form the basis of your discussion time.

All Examples Have Their Limits

Confession: I chose the book of James as my example because it easily lends itself to showing how the study method works. James is chock-full of all of the kinds of things you can annotate, it is fairly straightforward to interpret, and it is easy to apply. And it's not very long. Not all books are so accessible.

Bear in mind that if you are studying a lengthy book, your notes on the text may be much sparser than the ones in our example from James. Repeated words or ideas may take longer to pinpoint. Comprehension may consist of retelling major points of a sweeping historical narrative. Interpretation may consist of a few valiant attempts that end up missing the mark because of a lack of background information. Characters may behave in inexplicable ways, authors may cover confusing or seemingly dull topics, language and imagery may confuse. And forget trying to pronounce peoples' names.

If you encounter frustration or feel bogged down, remind yourself that your job as a student is to keep moving forward with the tools available. At different times, in different books, you will use each of the different study skills with varying degrees of effectiveness. But still use them. Still fight for your own personal contact with the text before looking to other sources for help. James would urge you to keep asking for wisdom, trusting that the Lord will give it, and remembering that your efforts are for the long term. Steadfastness in a student is a truly wonderful thing.

A Few Final Thoughts on Personal Study with the Five P's

So you've done it. You've walked through the text like a methodical student. Maybe your schedule didn't allow for daily contact with your study, or maybe some days you had less time than others, but you have used the time available to honor the Five P's. Will you allow me to throw in one bonus *P* for your consideration? If at all possible, share your study efforts with other *people.*

As I hinted at earlier, gathering with others to discuss your findings from personal study will greatly enhance your benefit from the work you have done. Bible study certainly does happen at a personal level, but within community it takes on dimension and accountability that it would not otherwise have. Studying with a partner or a group helps keep you moving forward, and it helps guard you against derailing into interpretations and applications that may not honor the text. If you are in a location or stage of life that makes gathering in a group difficult, personal study will definitely move you toward Bible literacy. But if at all possible, gather others to study with you. Your group will become the vehicle for discussion, confession, repentance, encouragement, and mutual edification. You will know the assurance that you're not the only one who finds study challenging, and you will share in the joy of discovery and understanding together.

Just as a group can serve as a reference point to keep you on the right track with your study, so also can sound teaching and preaching. These gifts to the body of believers are more accessible than ever before. Whether meeting in a group is possible for you or not, take advantage of the wealth of sound teaching available to you through online sources. If you're unsure who to listen to, ask your pastor whose teaching has been of personal help to him. Check what you're learning on your own against the teaching of trusted teachers. Just remember to use these resources *after* you have employed the Five P's in your personal study. Preaching and teaching take on greater dimension and accomplish far more when we come to them already saturated in the text they expound.

It is often true that avid students become avid teachers. I know this was the case for me. I was so excited to share the wealth of understanding I was uncovering that I soon moved from student to teacher. Of course, I didn't stop being a student—in many ways, beginning to teach was a means for keeping me accountable to study. Knowing that others were depending on me to show up prepared, and knowing that the Lord takes seriously the role of teacher (James 3:1), pressed me to become a far better student than I might ever have been on my own.

It is one thing to be a careful student, using the Five P's to guide your study, but it is another to be a careful teacher, guiding your students to learn and implement the Five P's. If you are a teacher, I offer some help in doing just that in the next chapter.

9

Help for Teachers

> Do your best to present yourself to God as one approved, a worker who has no need to be ashamed, rightly handling the word of truth.
>
> 2 Tim. 2:15

I am a terrible small group member. If you've ever been trained to lead a small group, I hope you've been offered this priceless nugget of advice: never make eye contact with the group member who wants to hijack the discussion. Your group is relying on you. If you look at her as you ask the next discussion question, it's game over.

I'm the one you never look at. Or at least, I used to be. Small group time was a nightmare for me and for everyone in my group. I would show up each week with my workbook marked to pieces with additional questions and insights I had discovered during my personal study. Discussion time was never long enough for me. I couldn't wait to get past "Joys and Concerns" so we could dig into the lesson. (I don't know your second cousin's mailman. Can we talk about Romans yet?) I was constantly thinking how I would have asked a question differently, what cross-reference I would have highlighted, how I would have taught a particular idea. I would sit on the edge of my seat, leaning in, waiting for the moment I could interject my observation or discovery into the conversation.

I remember the day I offered an alternative interpretation of the passage our study's author had covered. I had no idea silence could be so loud. Or so long. Generally speaking, women's small groups are places where consensus is prized. That gets nailed down in kindergarten. What on earth was wrong with me?

To all my former small group leaders out there, I apologize. If I were you, I would have wanted to thump me on the forehead. And to the leader who pulled me aside and said, "You know, I think you might have a teaching gift," I thank you from the bottom of my heart. Thank you for recognizing something in me that I couldn't see in myself.

Maybe you can relate to my experience. Maybe your small group leader avoids eye contact. Maybe you know that feeling of being about to explode all over your small group and have wondered if you're just a smarty-pants teacher's pet with a serious pride problem. Or maybe you have a spouse or accountability partner who is patiently enduring your weekly (nightly?) unloading of every single thing you are learning during your personal study time. It's important to ask yourself the pride question, but it's also important to consider the teaching question—especially if others have noticed evidence of a teaching gift in you.

Maybe the reason you're a bad group member is that you're wired to teach.

I hope you are. I believe the church desperately needs well-equipped women teachers, women who will handle Scripture with care and diligence and who have a heart for Bible literacy. It matters that women teach women, and that they do so with excellence. I believe it matters for three reasons.

Why Women Need Women Teachers

First, we need the *example* of women teachers. When a woman sees someone who looks like her and sounds like her teaching the Bible with passion and intelligence, she begins to recognize that she, too, can love God with her mind—perhaps beyond what she had thought necessary or possible. Had I only heard men teach the Bible well, I don't know that I would have considered myself capable of doing the same. Thankfully, God gave me smart, diligent women to set an example of what it means to open the Word with reverence and skill.

Second, we need the *perspective* of women teachers. A woman teacher will naturally gravitate toward application and examples that are accessible and recognizable to other women. Think: fewer football and action movie analogies, more HGTV and romantic comedy analogies; less about porn addiction or abdication of responsibility, more about self-image issues or sins of the tongue. A woman teacher will also lift different truths from a text than a man might. This is not to say she will feminize a text (a pitfall we will discuss further), but that she will emphasize those elements of the text that highlight the role of women in redemptive history, or that speak to sin issues women commonly face.

Third, we need the *authority* of women teachers. A woman can tell other women to stop making idols of their children or spouses in a way a man can't. A woman can address other women on vanity, pride, submission, and contentment in a way a man can't. Women teachers hold empathetic authority over their female students; we have the ability to say, "I understand the besetting sins and fears of womanhood, and I commend to you the sufficient counsel of Scripture."

So, by all means, ask yourself if the Lord is calling you to teach. The church needs women teaching women. And if his answer is "yes," gather a group and get going. But do so with care. The book of James warns us not to enter into teaching lightly, but to soberly consider that those who teach will be judged with greater strictness (James 3:1).

What does it look like to take the role of teaching lightly? I believe this happens when we confuse teaching with public speaking. They are not the same thing. Sometimes the church is slow to discern the difference between a gifted speaker and a gifted teacher. The speaker and the teacher rely on different sets of tools and have different objects in view. The speaker relies on rhetoric, storytelling, and humor to inspire and exhort. The teacher relies on knowledge, insight, and the ability to boil down the complex to the simple in order to train and instruct. The speaker makes fans, the teacher makes disciples.

We take the role of teacher lightly when we elevate the

tools of the public speaker over those of the teacher. I love humor and storytelling as much as the next person. I have used them in this book. But the teacher must constantly ask herself if she is relying on the tools of the speaker to the extent that the teaching content fades into the background. If people remember my stories and jokes but not my lesson, I have missed the mark. Ideally, a gifted teacher is also a gifted speaker. But if I have to choose one to take the platform, give me the teacher any day. The teacher will contend for Bible literacy.

So, how can we, as careful teachers, take the Five P's and train others to love and use them in their study? How can we craft lessons that honor the approach we have outlined? To do so will require us to prepare diligently, structure wisely, and teach responsibly.

Prepare Diligently

It goes without saying that in order to teach the Five P's, you must first use them yourself. Believe it or not, a teacher is most faithful to her students when she teaches them according to her own lack of understanding. I always believed that teachers taught because they knew more than their students. I no longer believe this to be the case. I teach because of what I don't know. I realize that the questions that occur to me as I read a passage are probably the questions that others are asking as well. The difference between me and others, between the teacher and the student, is that I can't leave those questions lying unexplored in the margins. If anything, the teacher is not the one with greater knowledge but with a greater natural curiosity to pursue the questions we all encounter. Because of her wiring, she is the one more ready to dig for understanding than her peers. Her enthusiasm for discovery becomes contagious among her students.

So I teach to learn. Knowing that my students need me to learn well helps me to prepare carefully. Careful preparation begins by putting into practice the Five P's, and when the time is right, distilling for my students the most important pieces of my own study time. In order to do this, a teacher must hold herself to the practice of consulting commentaries only after attempting comprehension, interpretation, and application on her own. Then she must choose her commentaries well. It takes time to know which authors are the most reliable. Once you find them, they tend to become your guiding stars. I have been known to choose a book of the Bible to study based on whether my favorite author has written a commentary on it.

As you begin building a list of trusted commentaries or authors, ask others for help: your pastor, another like-minded teacher, a seminary professor. Once you find an excellent author, read his or her sources. Follow the footnotes to see who shaped your author's thinking. Then read what those people wrote as well. The footnotes are a gold mine for finding additional sources to consult.

As we have noted, not all commentaries will say the same thing. When you find conflict among your trusted sources, look for where the most consensus lies and weigh that interpretation against your own understanding of the text. You may have to decide whether to teach the most common interpretation or the one you align with the closest. If it won't cause confusion, consider doing both. Acknowledge your own position to your students. Then tell them you are in the minority and faithfully present the prevailing view. Be sure to treat it with the thoroughness and fairness it deserves.

As you prepare, remember to document your sources in your notes. This will help you locate where an idea came from if someone asks you a question about it or if you need to revisit it yourself. I just write the author's last name and a page number in parentheses next to the thought I want to be able to locate again.

Thorough preparation requires a commitment of many hours. The amount of time you spend actually teaching a study is a fraction of the time you spend preparing. Your job is to absorb a large amount of information and then distill its most important elements for your students. Think of yourself as a professional organizer ordering an overflowing storage closet. You sort through piles of information, deciding what needs to be kept and where it should be kept, arranging and labeling so that a student can easily find and use it.

Structure Wisely

Not only does a teacher organize information so that it is accessible, she organizes the way it will be delivered. How you choose to structure your study will impact how much material you can cover and how deeply you can dig into the text. Will there be homework? Will you use your meeting time for prayer or discussion, or just for teaching? The structure of your study will determine its focus.

The study I lead meets for a two-hour window of small group discussion, worship, and teaching. Our group is large, so we require more structure than a group meeting in a home. In a home setting, the teaching might be interwoven with discussion, and the need for a schedule might be more flexible.

Many women's studies devote a significant portion of their time together to relationship-building elements like sharing prayer requests and icebreaker questions. These are needed elements, but they are also the ones most likely to eat up discussion and teaching time. If the women in your group have other opportunities to connect relationally (such as community groups or Sunday school), consider limiting this element during your meeting time. I tell my study participants up front that we very much want them to connect relationally, but that our primary goal is to grow their knowledge of and love for God. We guard small group time for discussion of the homework. We aren't rigid about it—we just keep it as our main focus. Prayer requests are written on note cards and e-mailed out to the group. If there is a specific need, we pray for it together in small group time. To build relationships, leaders often gather their groups for a meal at a time other than when the study meets. And we encourage women to linger and chat for as long as they like after the teaching.

Thoughts on Homework

If you are new to teaching, you may want to wait on writing a curriculum. You might begin by just asking the women in your group to read repetitively and annotate. You could then e-mail out a list of three or four interpretation and application questions for them to consider before you meet. I have found that at least some weekly homework is necessary to make the most of the time you will spend together. Whether you just ask the women to read repetitively or you assign them questions, do your best to withhold commentary until the discussion/teaching time. Structure your homework and teaching in such a way that it honors the learning process.

I write a curriculum for each study I teach. Each week the women read a section of the text and answer questions about it. The questions are heavily comprehension-based, with a few interpretation and application questions at regular intervals. The homework asks them to paraphrase, look up words in the dictionary, check cross-references, and read in alternate translations. My goal for the homework is that my students will come to the Bible study having spent time carefully absorbing what the text says (comprehension). During the study, we use group discussion and teaching time to explore together what the text means (interpretation) and how it should challenge us to be different (application). I actually intend the homework to raise almost as many questions as it answers, to lead women into a recognition of what they don't know. I then allow discussion time and teaching to resolve the dissonance the homework has created.

The homework questions contain very little commentary on my part; I do not provide many explanations or word meanings, unless absolutely necessary. This helps the student to develop the skill of questioning on her own and to learn not to fear the "not knowing" part of the learning process. We discuss the interpretation and application questions in the homework during small group time and/ or during the teaching. Each week's homework concludes with a reflection on what aspect of God's character has been revealed in the text, and how understanding that aspect of his character changes the way we think and act.

Writing effective homework requires the teacher to think like the student. As you begin your preparation, read through the text and note in the margins the questions that you would naturally have after reading it. Your students are likely to have the same questions. Remember that the question that seems obvious to you may actually be necessary for your students. Asking them to define words, count repeated words or phrases, or reiterate basic concepts helps train them to begin adopting those practices without the prompting of a curriculum. It helps them learn to study better on their own.

Also keep in mind the importance of asking the difficult question, the one you may even be afraid to ask yourself. This is the question that tempts you to say, "I'm just going to trust that to the Lord and move on." If the text talks about a father selling his daughter into slavery, ask your students in the homework how such a command could possibly come from a good and loving God. If the text describes Jesus advising you to cut off your hand to avoid sin, ask your students if Jesus is commanding self-mutilation. If you know that a passage is often pulled out of context, challenge the misuse:

"Does Philippians 4:13 mean we can do anything we set our minds to? Why or why not? Can you think of another passage that supports your answer?"

Assure your students that, even if they are unable to come up with a suitable answer, acknowledging the difficult question and attempting to answer it is part of reaching for understanding. Avoiding the difficult questions only feeds doubt and fear over the long term. Your students will find reassurance knowing that it is safe to ask the difficult questions, and that smart people have thought hard about them for over two millennia.

Writing curriculum is hard work. If possible, enlist the help of a friend for input and critique. Ask her to work through the homework and give you feedback on which questions helped and which were confusing or unhelpful. Often, a question that makes perfect sense to you may need to be reworded to make sense to others.

Laying out a study well requires the teacher to walk through the Five P's study method asking which parts of it would be difficult for someone just learning to use it. Will my students pay attention to this key word? Will they notice a repeated idea? Will they take a statement at face value that requires closer observation? Where will they be tempted to rush? Where are they likely to bog down?

Being able to pinpoint the answers to these questions and others like them requires us to continuously remind ourselves of how the text appeared to us the first time we encountered it. Once we have become familiar with a text, we can forget the questions and difficulties it originally posed for us. Good teachers are able to see the text through the eyes of their students. For this reason, I begin writing curriculum before I have done exhaustive study on a passage. This allows me to ask the most naturally occurring questions, to draw out the most basic observations before they become potentially obscured by a chorus of commentators. I refine and expand on the questions I have written after I have studied a bit.

This is where I differ from other approaches. I don't intend the homework to teach, per se. I intend the homework primarily to aid in comprehension and to begin the process of personal interpretation and application. Strictly speaking, teaching is commentary. My goal for the homework is that it would prepare the hearts and minds of my students for the teaching time. If they have done the work of personally attempting comprehension, interpretation, and application beforehand, they will hear my teaching with a far more perceptive ear—both for its strengths and its shortcomings. They will know when I have handled a text responsibly because they will have invested time grappling with it before coming to the group study. There is a high level of accountability in this, and I welcome it.

Remember, you don't have to create your own curriculum. You can use an existing curriculum that honors the learning process by offering minimal commentary and emphasizing comprehension, or you can ask your students to simply read repetitively as their preparation. Don't let intimidation over developing your own material hold you back from teaching. Not every teacher is a curriculum writer, but every teacher can take her students deeper into the Word by utilizing some form of homework to jump-start the learning process.

Teach Responsibly

Teaching a passage to those who have studied it is far more demanding than teaching one to those who have not. My hope is that the homework will challenge their thinking enough that by the time they hear me teach, they won't just take my word for it. Knowing that they will think critically about my teaching holds me accountable to avoid seven common teaching pitfalls.

1. Hopping Around

Have you ever settled in to hear a teaching on a key text, only to have the teacher read through the passage briefly before spending forty minutes ricocheting around the entire Bible? A student who has spent a week parsing a chapter of Ephesians will not be satisfied if the teacher uses the key text merely as a launch pad. She will want to linger there, as she should. She will have discovered that the text at hand is worthy of forty undistracted minutes of the group's time, that those forty minutes will probably not be enough time to resolve her questions on that text alone.

Good teaching will necessarily involve the use of cross-references, but not at the expense of the primary text. We teachers are prone to wander, particularly when our primary text is a difficult one. The teacher who strives to build Bible literacy needs to stay put. Her primary goal is not to show how the key text relates to a thousand other passages, but to teach the key text so thoroughly that it will come to mind automatically when a student encounters similar themes elsewhere in her study.

2. Feminizing the Text

Women who teach women the Bible are constantly faced with the temptation to take a passage and overlay it with a meaning unique to womanhood. Any time we take a passage that is aimed at teaching *people* and teach it as though it is aimed specifically at *women*, we run the risk of feminizing a text.

This is not to say that we can't look for gender-specific application points from a text that speaks to both genders. Rather, we have to guard against offering interpretation and application that rob the text of its original intent by focusing too exclusively on a gender-specific framework. The book of Ruth is not a book about women for women, any more than the book of Jude is a book about men for men. The Bible is a book about God, written for people. By all means, teach Psalm 139 as it relates to women and body image, but resist the urge to teach it exclusively so. It is not the job of the female teacher to make the Bible relevant or palatable to women. It is her job to teach the text responsibly. A female teacher will sometimes bring a different perspective to the text than a male teacher because of her gender, but not always. A student who has spent time in the text before hearing teaching on it will know when the text is being feminized.

3. Wild Extrapolation

In the interest of "bringing the text to life," teachers sometimes succumb to the temptation of adding a little paint around the edges of the canvas of Scripture. I admit that it is interesting to speculate about the unrecorded thoughts and motives of Mary, the mother of Jesus. It is perhaps even beneficial to a point. But at some point it moves from being helpful to being distracting, and potentially to being extrabiblical.

If you have ever watched a movie adaptation of a familiar Bible story, you will understand this point—the more literate you are about what the Bible actually says about the exodus, the less you will be able to enjoy Cecil B. DeMille's extrapolation of it. Imagining beyond the text holds great appeal for an audience, but limited appeal for a student. Familiarity with a text prior to hearing it taught moves the participant from audience member to student. A student who has spent a week immersed in the text you are teaching will know when you go "off script."

4. Overdependence on Storytelling or Humor

In order to be relatable and engaging, teachers employ storytelling and humor as rhetorical devices. This is not wrong. Humor and storytelling humanize the teacher, help keep listeners engaged, and make teaching points memorable. It is not okay for a teacher to be unrelatable, boring, or forgettable. But it's also not okay for a teacher to become overreliant on humor and storytelling, or to use them in a way that manipulates or distracts from the lesson. If they don't reinforce the teaching, they will compromise it.

If someone were to break down your teaching into a pie chart, how much of the pie would be taken up with these two elements? If you asked your students to tell you one thing they remembered from your lesson, would they recall a key point or a funny story? Audiences love humor and stories, whether they support the message or not. Students love sound content made more memorable by a well-placed illustration or quip. A well-prepared student will know whether her teacher uses these rhetorical devices as filler or as reinforcement.

5. Pandering to Emotion

When I read Scripture aloud from the platform, I frequently cry. I'm not sure why, other than that I find the truths in the text deeply moving. It used to frustrate me, but the Lord is showing me that teaching the Bible should involve the emotions. That is, teaching the Bible should awaken in both the teacher and the student a deeper love for God, one that profoundly affects our emotions. Loving God with our minds should result in loving God with our hearts deeply and purely.

We run into trouble when we intentionally target peoples' emotions for the sake of creating a shared experience. It is tempting to craft a lesson that begins with a joke and ends with a tear-jerking story. Why? Because it's a rhetorical formula that works. Sometimes listeners confuse being inspired by the Holy Spirit with being manipulated by a well-crafted human message.

How can we tell the difference? It isn't always easy, but here is one thought: The emotional manipulator will increase your *love for her* as much as or more than she increases your *love for God*. A teacher's job is to draw attention to the beauty of the text, not create a shared experience that is moving. Her job is to extol the God of the Bible, not build a cult of personality. A well-prepared student is less susceptible to emotional manipulation.

6. Overpacking the Teaching

One of the biggest challenges of crafting a lesson is knowing what content to include and what to leave out. It takes time to develop a feel for how much content you can reasonably address during your teaching time. Initially, most teachers make the mistake of overpreparing. This can lead to getting bogged down in a sea of notes or keeping your students far longer than you intended. Most people don't enjoy drinking from a fire hose, so while it's okay to have more notes than you can teach through, it's important to have a contingency plan of what you will cut if time runs short.

Here, again, the teacher whose students have already spent time in the key text has an advantage. The work of comprehension they have already invested frees you up to explore interpretation and application without having to lay extensive groundwork. You are extending and reinforcing their understanding, rather than starting from scratch. A well-prepared student will not require an overpacked teaching time.

7. Playing the Expert

Nobody likes to feel stupid, least of all, the teacher. Because of this, teachers are sometimes reluctant to admit the limits to their knowledge. Be honest about your limitations: it's okay for the teacher to say, "I don't know." In fact, it can be reassuring to your students. Practice full disclosure when more than one interpretation is widely accepted for a passage. Give an honest answer that acknowledges differing views. This gives your students an opportunity to think through which view fits best with their own reading of the text. A well-prepared student knows that a difficult passage requires care. She will know if you have given a simple answer to a complex issue. Far better to be honest about your confidence (or lack of) in a particular interpretation.

The best part of teaching women a text they have previously studied is that it holds the teacher accountable not to "wing it." The prepared student can spot shallow preparation on the part of the teacher. Asking more from my students up front means my students can and should ask more of me during the teaching.

Why Teaching with the Five P's Is Liberating

Though teaching is hard work, using a method like the Five P's significantly lightens the load. The beauty of using the Five P's is that it frees the teacher from deciding what topics to address. Her lesson is determined by the content of the passage at hand. I find great comfort in knowing that the text will introduce what is needful, when it is needful, in a context that will display it to best advantage. All I have to do is teach the next verse. Teaching a topic requires me to develop elaborate outlines connecting the dots from many passages. Teaching with the Five P's allows the text to be my outline.

I agree with James: not many should presume to teach. Shaping someone's understanding of the things of God is a huge responsibility, and it is not to be taken lightly. There is no room for a "fake it 'til you make it" mentality among those who would desire to teach. Those who take their role seriously will give hours to preparing, teach for forty minutes, and spend hours mulling over what more they might have said, what else they could have explained, and what illustration they should have used. When a young woman tells me, "I want to teach like you," I always think, "I must have made it look too easy." Teaching, like other callings, is certainly not easy, but if the Lord has wired you to do it, you can trust he will supply you with the means.

Conclusion

Seek His Face

> You have said, "Seek my face." My heart says to you, "Your face, Lord, do I seek."
>
> Ps. 27:8

Someone asked me recently, after learning I was a Bible teacher, if I was a God-worshipper or a Bible-worshipper. The question didn't come as a complete surprise. When you spend as much time as I do asking people to care about knowing their Bibles, someone is bound to ask if you have lost sight of the forest for the trees. My answer was simple: I want to be conformed to the image of God. How can I become conformed to an image that I never behold? I am not a Bible-worshipper, but I cannot truly be a God-worshipper without loving the Bible deeply and reverently. Otherwise, I worship an unknown god.

A Bible-worshipper loves an object. A God-worshipper loves a person. We can love the Bible with our minds, but we cannot love it with our hearts any more than we can love a car or a cappuccino. An object cannot receive or reciprocate love. Only a person can do that. So if you have read this book in an effort to love the Bible more, I want to applaud you and caution you at the same time. Please do learn to love God with your mind through the faithful study of his Word, but please don't attach your affections to anything less than the person of God himself. Our study of the Bible is only beneficial insofar as it increases our love for the God it proclaims. Bible study is a means to an end, not an end in and of itself. It is a means to love God more, and to live differently because we have learned to behold him better. And it is a means to become what we behold. The reciprocal love of God is a love that transforms.

In John 13, Jesus tells his disciples that their influence will be recognizable. He tells them that the world will know them for a distinct reason: their love for one another. Your love for others is the overflow of your love for God. Your love for God will increase as you learn to know him better. But never lose sight that your influence will be noticed in how you use your heart, not your head. Bible literacy that does not transform is a chasing after the wind. Christians will be known by our love, not our knowledge.

We will not be known for just any kind of love—we will be known for the kind of love the Father has shown to us, and that we in turn show to others.

We Become What We Behold

When I was in the seventh grade, I wanted to be just like my friend Meg. Meg had glossy blond hair that fell into a perfect pageboy. She had enviable clothes. She was funny, smart, and popular. She listened to cool music and carried the right purse. She had a figure, and a tan the color of honey. She knew things about makeup. She was pretty much perfection.

So I did what lots of middle school girls do: I got a pageboy haircut. I scoured the clearance racks for Meg-like clothes that I could afford with my babysitting money. I changed my speech patterns and musical tastes to match hers. I even tried to learn to walk with the same stride she had. I studied everything that made Meg wonderful and then tried to imitate it to the smallest detail. Never mind that I was six inches taller than she was, with pale, freckled skin and all the curviness of a ten-year-old boy. I made an in-depth study of her, and I did everything in my power to conform to her image.

I have often thought about this time in my life, both for what I did wrong and for what I did right. I was actually very good at recognizing what it took to effectively imitate someone—paying careful attention to her attributes. And I was even right to want to imitate perfection. But I was wrong to think I could find it in another human.

We humans are imitators. From the time we are babies, we imitate those around us. Sometimes we imitate actively, like when I tried to become Meg. Other times we imitate passively, like when we realize belatedly that we are turning into our mothers. Could it be that we are designed this way for a reason? That our propensity to imitate is actually intended for our good?

Ephesians 5:1 tells us to "be imitators of God, as dearly

loved children." Children who know they are dearly loved imitate their parents out of joyful adoration. They *want* to be like them. And this is the way we are called to imitate our perfect God: not out of a slavish middle-school desire to become better or different than we currently are, but out of a joyful recognition that he is lovely and completely worthy of imitation.

But know this: we will not imitate him by accident. We will certainly become our mothers without so much as trying, but we will not wake up ten years from now and find we have passively taken on the character of God.

Active Imitation

Imitation of God happens in much the same way that it did in junior high, only this time, we have a much worthier object. Just as I made a study of my friend, we must make a study of our God: what he loves, what he hates, how he speaks and acts. We cannot imitate a God whose features and habits we have never learned. We must make a study of him if we want to become like him. We must seek his face.

There are many good reasons to invest in learning God's Word, but there is none better than this: that with every *purposeful* effort, with every *perspective*-laced reading, with every *patient* step forward, with each *process*-ordered attempt, with every *prayer*-infused interlude in the pages of Scripture, we move closer to his countenance, we come more directly in line with the radiance of his face. We see him for who he is, which is certainly a reward in itself, but it is a reward with the secondary benefit of being forever altered by the vision.

We become what we behold. Do you believe that? Whether passively or actively, we become conformed to the pattern we spend the most time studying.

Upon what is your gaze fixed? Your bank account? Your bathroom scale? Your child's next accolade? Your dream kitchen? The latest blockbuster TV series? Your phone? It is the nature of this life that we must fight daily to make room in our line of sight for that-which-transcends. Many things hold a legitimate claim on our attention, but when our eyes are free from the two-year-old or the spreadsheet or the textbook or the dinner dishes, where do we turn them? If we spend our time gazing only on lesser things, we will become like them, measuring our years in terms of human glory.

But here is good news: the One whom we most need to behold has made himself known. He has traced with a fine hand the lines and contours of his face. He has done so in his Word. We must search for that face, though babies continue to cry, bills continue to grow, bad news continues to arrive unannounced, though friendships wax and wane, though both ease and difficulty weaken our grip on godliness, though a thousand other faces crowd close for our affection, and a thousand other voices clamor for our attention. By fixing our gaze on that face, we trade mere human glory for holiness: "Beholding the glory of the Lord, [we are] transformed into the same image from one degree of glory to another" (2 Cor. 3:18).

There are really only two possibilities in this life: be conformed to the image of God or be conformed to the pattern of this world. No doubt, you want the former. But be warned: The Word is living and active. It will conform you by dividing you. And in the dividing, miracle of miracles, it will render you whole. We become what we behold. I don't know about you, but I have much "becoming" to do. There is a vastness between what I am and what I ought to be, but it is a vastness able to be spanned by the mercy and grace of him whose face it is most needful for me to behold. In beholding God we become like him.

So make a faithful study of the One you want to imitate, as a dearly loved child. Study everything that makes God wonderful and mimic to your heart's delight, as the joyful expression of your reciprocal love for him. Respond as David did: "My heart says to you, 'Your face, Lord, do I seek'" (Ps. 27:8). To the one that seeks him, the Lord is pleased to lift up his countenance, both now and forever. Study well the contours of his face. Let gazing on his loveliness touch mind and heart. And be transformed.

Recommended Resources

Help for Developing a Reliable Study Method

Kay Arthur, David Arthur, and Pete De Lacey. *The New How to Study Your Bible*. Eugene, OR: Harvest House, 2010.

Kathleen Buswell Nielson. *Bible Study: Following the Ways of the Word*. Phillipsburg, NJ: P&R, 2011.

John MacArthur. *How to Study the Bible*. Chicago: Moody, 2009.

Robert H. Stein. *A Basic Guide to Interpreting the Bible: Playing by the Rules*. 2nd ed. Grand Rapids, MI: Baker Academic, 2011.

Basic Tools for Bible Study

ESV Study Bible. Wheaton, IL: Crossway, 2011.

The New Bible Dictionary, edited by I. Howard Marshall, A. R. Miller, J. I. Packer, and D. J. Wiseman. 3rd ed. Downers Grove, IL: InterVarsity Press, 1996.

Choosing Reliable Commentaries

Keith Mathison. "Top Commentaries on Every Book of the Bible." Available on Ligonier's website: http://www.ligonier.org/blog/top-commentaries-on-every-book-of-the-bible/.

Inductive Studies for Almost Every Book of the Bible

LifeChange Bible study series. Colorado Springs, CO: NavPress.

Additional Reading on Metanarrative

Justin Buzzard. *The Big Story: How the Bible Makes Sense Out of Life*. Chicago: Moody, 2013.

On the Attributes of God

A. W. Pink. *The Attributes of God*. Available at http://www.pbministries.org/books/pink/Attributes/.

A. W. Tozer. *The Knowledge of the Holy*. New York: Harper, 1961.

Free Online Study Aids

Blue Letter Bible. Available at www.blueletterbible.org.

BibleGateway. Available at www.biblegateway.com.

Dictionary of Bible Themes. Compiled by Martin Manser, Alister McGrath, J. I. Packer, and D. J. Wiseman. Available on Bible Gateway at http://www.biblegateway.com/resources/dictionary-of-bible-themes/toc.

For the Auditory Learner, or for Those Who Find Repetitive Reading a Challenge

Download the free YouVersion app to your smartphone and listen to a book of the Bible while you exercise or drive, or anytime you might listen to music.

For an Extensive Examination of the Role of the Mind in Christian Devotion

J. P. Moreland. *Love Your God with All Your Mind: The Role of Reason in the Life of the Soul*. Revised and expanded edition. Colorado Springs, CO: NavPress, 2012.

Notes

Foreword

1. Edmund P. Clowney, *The Unfolding Mystery: Discovering Christ in the Old Testament* (Phillipsburg, NJ: P&R, 1988), 11.

Chapter 1: Turning Things Around

1. "What Do We Value Most?" NPR Radio TED Radio Hour, May 25, 2012, 14:00, http://www.npr.org/player/v2/mediaPlayer.html?action=1&t=3&islist=true&id=57&d=04-27-2012.
2. "Paul Bloom: The Origins of Pleasure," TED Talks, July 2011, http://www.ted.com/talks/paul_bloom_the_origins_of_pleasure.html.

Chapter 2: The Case for Bible Literacy

1. Vorjack, "Women Leaving the Church," *Patheos*, August 5, 2011, http://www.patheos.com/blogs/unreasonablefaith/2011/08/women-leaving-the-church/.

Chapter 4: Study with Perspective

1. Tom Mueller, "Underground Rome," *The Atlantic Monthly*, April 1997, http://www.theatlantic.com/past/docs/issues/97apr/rome.htm.
2. Stephan Faris, "Rome's Developing Subway," *Travel and Leisure*, April 2008, http://www.travelandleisure.com/articles/romes-developing-subway.
3. *Merriam-Webster OnLine*, s.v. "literature," http://www.merriam-webster.com/dictionary/literature?show=0&t=1385582790.
4. Gordon Fee and Douglas Stuart, *How to Read the Bible for All Its Worth* (Grand Rapids, MI: Zondervan, 1993), 74.

Chapter 5: Study with Patience

1. *A League of Their Own*, 1992. "There's no crying in baseball!"

Scripture Index

Download a free study guide for *Women of the Word* at

crossway.org/WilkinStudy

For additional resources from Jen Wilkin, including information on her Bible study curriculum, visit

jenwilkin.net